and then there were three

sixty-seven letters to Sasha

and then there were three

sixty-seven letters to Sasha

(second edition)

By Julie G. Fox

Published by The Invisible Imprint in the United Kingdom in 2024
First edition published by Dog Ear Publishing in 2015

ISBN: 978-1-83919-665-2

To everyone who dares to love openly and authentically, despite the odds. And to the LGBTQ+ community worldwide—may our stories continue to inspire change and acceptance.

'Beloved' – too theatrical; 'lover' – too frank; 'friend' – too vague. Heartless country!

– Marina Tsvetaeva

1

Dear Sasha,

In the last scene of *El Sexo de los Ángeles*, a Spanish film about ménage à trois, a young couple finally figures out that it is a much more pleasant affair to accept their bisexual lover in their relationship than to fight over him, and they are subsequently enjoying a leisurely morning of waking side by side, all three of them taking turns making coffee and dancing half-dressed – young, beautiful, photogenic, their future lacking old-fashioned stereotyping about that sort of thing. It is all quite different in real life, assuming the three get past wanting to strangle each other. If they succeed in getting thus far, lots of pleasant, half-dressed mornings become possible…with coffee, pain au chocolat or plain toast with jam. But I am getting a little ahead of myself. As the three of us, dear Sasha, were part of a real trio, living an otherwise uneventful life in central London, I would like to recreate our story bit by bit while you are waking up some 3,318

1

kilometres – according to Google Maps – away from George and me.

I don't think I ever had a chance to tell you how I found out that George was bi-curious back in his university years. On what seemed like an ordinary morning five years ago, I waited until I heard the familiar sound of the post dropping to the floor through the letterbox, climbed out of bed and collected the new issue of *The Economist*, together with the electric bill and British Heart Foundation pamphlet announcing the opening of a new furniture and electricals shop. I stood in the kitchen and undressed *The Economist* from its plastic cover, and I was about to place it on the counter when George grabbed the magazine out of my hands. Its headline exclaimed GAY ACTIVISTS IN UKRAINE FACE CRIMINAL CHARGES.

'Since when are you so passionate about gay rights in Ukraine?' I raised my eyebrow, sipping coffee from George's enormous white mug.

'I loved a Ukrainian.' George looked up from the magazine.

You see, dear Sasha, George and I have always been in the habit of sharing our memories of youth with one another rather freely; thus, I didn't even think of making any fuss about George's comment at all, but I did praise him on bedding a lesbian. He looked up at me with a faint smile and said that he was actually referring to a gay male friend.

2

And that is how it all started. With a bit of buttered toast getting stuck in my throat. With a two-minute coughing stint. With me finding out that you, dear Sasha, were living somewhere where your friends with alternative sexual orientations suffered greatly and were forced to stay 'in the closet', all at a time when our next-door neighbours, a young gay couple, were kissing each other goodbye every morning on the porch of our block of flats in plain view of the whole neighbourhood, with nobody giving it a second thought. The story started with the idea that we had to save you, dear Sasha. I had to save you, as I am usually the one who goes out and saves people while George makes a living.

George is now fully awake, coming up to me and placing a quick peck on my cheek while I am typing away. He is about to start our coffee routine, much more boring now that you are gone. We do not dance naked while making coffee on most mornings. We don't dance at all any more.

2

Dear Sasha,

It took me a few years to find you, as you happen to have a rather common name, and for about a year or two, we made contact with at least a couple of dozen Sashas with the same surname as yours, who responded to my queries with the typical 'Sorry, I am not the Sasha you are looking for.' It was not until I actually contacted the alumni association of the university where you and George met that we had a breakthrough with a friend of a friend of a friend in possession of your mobile number.

Your first conversation with George was very emotional. I left the room, knowing that there were certain things the two of you wanted to say to each other that you would not want anyone to overhear. It wasn't until your fourth or fifth conversation that I actually asked George to let me listen in, albeit without understanding a word of what was said, as the two of you were conversing in a mixture of two languages I did not understand. When I did edge closer to George's computer and saw you on the screen, I stopped breathing for a split second. I am not sure whether it was the fact that on that warm evening in May your shirt was unbuttoned all the way down, whether it was your blue eyes staring intently at the camera with such sorrow and longing, whether it was your hollow voice and the way you started your sentences in French and seamlessly ended them in German, or whether it was your French accent, so different from all the other accents I had heard, so very angular and so distinctly un-French. Or all of the above, perhaps. I felt a sudden sharp pain under my left breast, had to grab the back of the chair George was sitting on for some stability and then resumed my breathing as normal. However, dear Sasha, I was not the same person upon disconnecting.

3

Dear Sasha,

I saw you for the first time within a few months of our first Skype experience. I planned a reunion with your and George's French teacher at her family home in the south of France, without giving much thought to what would happen once we met in person but rather concentrating on such mundane things as visas, hotel bookings and flight schedules.

We flew in within hours of each other, and the entire evening, the party – which included the French teacher's grown-up children, their partners and even some neighbours from around the corner – communicated entirely in a language I enjoyed listening to but was hardly proficient in. I caught a few words here and there, getting an idea of what the conversation was all about without being able to enjoy the details. I spent the evening listening to the sound of it while drinking wine and eating lots of different kinds of cheeses covered with drops of sweat, as the heat was unbearable in that last week of September. Gainsbourg was singing in the background. The room was full of smoke, from the vintage Russian Belomorkanal to American Marlboro. You had a lot to drink, dear Sasha, remember? You were eyeing one of the male guests – a friend of the teacher's son, I think, although I cannot quite remember now.

The party grew fairly quickly as the news spread in the neighbourhood about the teacher's foreign students showing up. I was sitting in a corner with the only English-language book I could locate in the house. The reading lamp was a little bent to one side, and the lampshade left a large brown stain on the yellow page. You could not see my face, but I could watch yours, animated, your thin lips moving distinctly and articulating every word just as you would juggle them, throwing them up one after another, catching them and stacking them in a tall pile. Your cigarette drew strange zigzags. Your eyes shifted around the room ever so noticeably, never giving away your real emotion after pausing briefly on each of the guests. At that moment, dear Sasha, I so wanted to be a man.

4

Dear Sasha,

Have I ever had a chance to tell you that when I was a child, I wanted to be a boy, all the way through my early teens until just around the time when I started my first period? After that, I switched to wanting boys instead of wanting to be one. I remember having fights with my mother about not wanting to wear a skirt beyond the mandatory school uniform dress. I wore trousers. All kinds. Jeans. Shorts. Even at my wedding, I wore a trouser suit!

That boyish look that I assumed around the time I met you definitely had something to do with the fact that you fancied men. And I, unfortunately, was a woman. I wore jeans. Boots. I started smoking. I cut my hair even shorter than it had been before. 'Boy short,' I told my hairdresser, Paul, the week before we were to travel to the French reunion. My handbag was replaced by a backpack. I did leave the earrings and the brass matryoshka locket under the ripped T-shirt; however, I did have B cups under that T-shirt. So, dear Sasha, you were not attracted to me there in France. You were not. For the whole ten days of us staying there.

On our way back home, on the train ride between Paris and Berlin, where you were to catch a plane back home, there was a breakthrough. It was a night train. We had two bunks. Two beds at the top. Two at the bottom. There were just the three of us in the cabin. Remember? George was marching up and down the train carriage, trying to get an elusive 3G connection that kept disappearing. You and I were finishing up a bottle of vodka that we had opened merely two hours earlier. I probably did end up looking like a boy in the fog created by lots of booze and non-stop partying the days before, because when I leaned towards you, Sasha, to tell you a joke, you pulled me closer and kissed me. I remember being paralysed by your kiss for a split second, and then my hands started moving in ways I couldn't control, ending up under your T-shirt and around your waist. My fingers ran below your belt; I felt your erection on my thigh as we moved closer to each other and hugged tightly. I remember that the whole episode lasted less than a minute. We jumped away from each other once we heard the sound of steps on the other side of the door. It wasn't George, and no one walked in, but we did not resume anything. We were both in shock about what had happened. Dear Sasha, I was in love with a gay man – you. And you had just got an erection while kissing me, a woman.

5

Dear Sasha,

Now, where did George come into all of this? And why hadn't I noticed much happening between you, dear Sasha, and George at all in the ten days we all spent together in France? Why didn't I even question whether anything at all could happen between you and George? You were lovers twenty-five years ago. It was more than a one-night stand. You wrote to each other after you graduated, and the last time you saw each other, you ended up being intimate. The last time you saw each other was the day of your wedding, dear Sasha. To a woman.

This might surprise a young, modern-day gay person living in one of the liberal countries of the Western world, but the older generation of gay Westerners will take in this information without blinking. The majority of gay men did end up marrying women as recently as the 1990s in the unorthodox West as well as in the traditional East.

In the former territories of the Soviet Union, such behaviour was not only understandable but the only one affording self-preservation and a sense of social stability. Homosexuality was illegal in the former Communist states – surprisingly, not at the hands of the first Communist leader following the revolution, as I would have imagined it to be. According to your careful research, the new Communist Party legalised homosexual activity in the former territories of the Russian Empire, and openly gay people were even allowed to serve in the government. In the 1930s, however, homosexuality was recriminalised. Some blamed the Church; others, the homophobic dictators of the times. Thus, having a boyfriend or girlfriend of the same sex in the Communist Bloc could land one in jail or in a psychiatric unit of an isolated hospital for 'political prisoners', which was the usual place for those who had any kind of disagreement with the ruling party's opinions on things not necessarily related to politics.

Following the dismemberment of the Soviet Union, most of the former Soviet countries did get a dose of Western freedom of choice in both sexual orientation and political opinion; however, the 'gay' subject was still a taboo in some places. Gay people of the former Communist Bloc lived in fear of verbal and physical harassment, having no protection from government institutions whatsoever; thus, a majority of gay people remained in the closet – you, dear Sasha, and your friends included.

6

Dear Sasha,

Talking about blending in, marrying a woman while fancying men, going to church while questioning the existence of God…I remember you telling me, dear Sasha, that you go to church on a regular basis and closely follow the holiday rituals, including some that got me quite suspicious that you become a very different person once you cross the border. I cannot for the life of me imagine you, my dear night owl, waking up in the early hours of the morning, before sunrise, to attend a church service. You have lived in fear, and while playing the role of a hardworking, churchgoing family man, you worked for your day-to-day survival. Through the years, it affected your psyche in ways that astonish me. In some of our conversations, you even manage to dissociate yourself from homosexual men altogether. Apparently, dear Sasha, as I have found out, it is quite a common psychological trait found in gay people all over the world, but it is more common in countries with repressive regimes. This dissociation –

you do not even think of yourself as gay but a 'normal' heterosexual man who once in a while likes to sleep with other men.

7

Dear Sasha,

Months after you were already gone, I spoke to a prominent German gay activist who, when the gay parade of 2013 was banned in Kyiv, flew to Ukraine to join a few dozen other activists to march along a narrow road near the Shuliavska metro station. All of them nearly got arrested but were quickly evacuated, fearing outbursts of aggression from the locals.

You have never participated in any marches, of course. And you told me once, dear Sasha, that you even encouraged a young friend who admitted to his family that he was gay to 'stop ruining his life' and 'get married to a nice girl'. You told me that you had witnessed the fates of old, lonely gay men too many times, and you felt sorry for them. You told me that one has to grow old surrounded by children and grandchildren. And that is exactly what you were planning to do.

8

Dear Sasha,

I have been writing all morning, listening to the seagulls. My coffee is already cold, with the milk that coloured the coffee beige starting to look more like an oil spill on its surface. I want a fresh cup but am too busy to get up, so I continue sipping the cold one with disgust.

I remember our mornings when you and George would strike up a conversation while waiting for the kettle to boil, about something that had nothing to do with how the three of us ended the previous evening. I remember I used to wear your or George's T-shirt on those mornings, my old grey jogging bottoms and fuzzy white cat slippers. My short hair unbrushed, I would interrupt my typing to look up and admire you, dear Sasha, standing there with your shirt unbuttoned, and I would stare at you for what seemed like an eternity, until I remembered that I had yet to do laundry that day, that I had yet to do anything that day, as I had spent all morning writing. I often try to go back in my memory to these mornings, dear Sasha, when I would slowly grow more aware of your conversation with George while still fogged by lack of sleep and rainy, grey weather. You would talk current politics and then switch to Tube strikes and then to the weather and the price of airline tickets.

Airlines. We flew constantly in the first few months after we had found you, dear Sasha. I remember being jet-lagged and tired quite a bit, but the excitement of you, this newly found friend, made the exhaustion more tolerable. We at first had to struggle with your restrictions on travel, as you were only able to fly visa-free to a handful of countries. I remember that the second time I saw you, George and I had to fly to Odessa, the seaside resort in southern Ukraine, which sits on the Black Sea, just north of Turkey. The once glamorous and proud city was quite ruined through the country's economic sufferings.

Odessa is the creation of a French general, a Belgian engineer, a half-Spanish, half-Irish admiral and a French nobleman. All four of them met quite by chance on a Russian military vessel in the 1770s and later on managed to convince Catherine the Great to establish the city. A Mediterranean city, it has been deprived of the necessary funds to keep all the art nouveau, Renaissance, and classicist buildings in proper condition, thanks to Ukraine's staggering economy, thus scaring the pedestrians with the occasional piece of wall or balcony falling on the pavements right in front of them.

Although we did not care much about the dilapidated state of the apartment complex we rented during our stay in Odessa, with smashed letterboxes and graffiti-covered walls inside and outside the building, it did take George and me some time to get used to the smell of the feline urine all around the building. It was the end of September. The air was still very warm, the buzzing of the mosquitoes – annoying, their biting habits – unbearable. I remember not sleeping very well at all the first night. I was intermittently woken up by a painful bite and the itching that ensued, and just when I fell asleep, you would start your snoring routine, dear Sasha, and I had to nudge you with my elbow to make sure you did some tossing and turning and hopefully stopped snoring for just enough time for the silence to be broken by another buzzing mosquito.

I woke up that first morning with my nose swollen from bites, my head spinning, and feeling dazed from the multitude of emotions that were surrounding the experience. The sun was pouring through the window. The noise of the cars and loud arguing of the local residents under the windows all sounded like a very odd film that was missing subtitles. I stared at your bare back, dear Sasha, as you were sitting at the kitchen table in front of your laptop. George was sitting next to you. Your hand was on George's thigh. Resting.

Your voices were low so as not to wake me up. I remember the feeling of warmth in my lower stomach as I watched the palm of your hand adjust its position to George's knee. I never realised this could have such an effect on me. I closed my eyes quickly, trying to figure out what exactly I was experiencing. Not only was I curious about the physical relationship between you and George, but it apparently excited me.

Whether something happened between the two of you that morning or not, dear Sasha, I will never know. I never bothered asking. I realised very quickly that it did not matter. It did, and it didn't. What mattered was that all three of us were getting very close to one another. It was the catching up. And laughing. And watching films, primarily gay romance, or rarely, as these are rare, films like El Sexo de los Ángeles, in which a girl joined up with a gay duo – or I think it was the other way around: the gay chap joined the heterosexual couple, or so the couple believed until the gay chap kissed the boy and then kissed the girl. And so in our case, George and I were also both kissed in turns. By you.

9

Dear Sasha,

Since almost the first day we met, I heard so much from you about the two years you and George dated in your early twenties. The stories poured out almost immediately when you realised that I had no issues with homosexuality in general nor with George's bisexuality in particular. And the stories were getting richer and richer in detail as time went by, either because we were becoming rather open with each other about our emotions and desires or because your imagination, dear Sasha, was taking flight, as George claimed at the time that he did not remember half of it. You were so good with stories. You could talk for hours. Drink. Smoke. Talk. I could listen to you for hours. Drink. Smoke. Listen. Once in a while, I would interrupt you with a question or a comment or a story of my own, usually remembering my own affairs with men.

It was always about men with you, dear Sasha. You told me you had always been attracted to men since you were young. And back in the time and place in which you grew up, just like for most gay men of your generation, the realisation that one was attracted to members of the same sex was not a pleasant one. Society was not on your side. And so your stories, dear Sasha, were all locked up in your head until a bottle of vodka and a long distance from your motherland freed up your memory and let you pour the contents of it right out on my lap. These were the stories of your multiple crushes at university – with George being one of the most memorable, of course. There were others. Most of them, if not all, were heterosexual young men who in moments of weakness or alcoholic haziness let you enjoy their bodies. And you were very modest in your asking. Sometimes a hug was all that was required to make you happy. The kind that you would recall the details of in a masturbation session before falling asleep that night. However, it was a much more intimate experience with George and a couple of others, as apparently even heterosexual men are sometimes so starved of sexual attention and so pressed for quick relief that they would gladly, if shyly, let you finish them off one way or another. This does not make them gay, of course. It makes them bi-curious young men happy to find quick relief.

10

Dear Sasha,

I knew you were once married. You married just like so many other homosexual men did in your time, because there was no other way to survive in society but to prove that you were 'normal'. There were places – bars, restaurants, public toilets – where gay men were known to congregate and find each other. Some were keeping long- or short-distance relationships going for years while married to unsuspecting women who just didn't think much of their husbands' absence of sexual desire. These topics were taboo. So whether your husband had sex with you once a month or once a year, you were to cook him meals and raise his kids, and depending on your hubby's personality and temper, you were free to keep a lover. I'm not sure whether your wife ever knew. Most likely, she suspected something.

Women were not your idea of a good time, although you told me that you did bed a few, but all of it was in an effort to conform to society's expectations. A few times, I am sure you just happened to have an erection, and an admiring female was ready to help you get rid of the pressure. When a young man's hormones are raging, sometimes it doesn't matter whether the recipient of one's affection is exactly of the right sex.

Is that what you felt, dear Sasha, when you had sex with me with your eyes shut and your thoughts drifting away, imagining a man's body or invoking memories of past male lovers? Did you have to feel George's hand on your behind in order to penetrate me? Did you ejaculate thinking about George? Mark? David? Others? I asked myself these questions often, when the mornings were grey and rainy, when I had a faint stomach ache because of something I had eaten the day before, or because my period was coming, or because I remembered how I used to kiss your neck, dear Sasha, while placing my hands on your shoulders and how you used to freeze for an instant and then look up at me from whatever you were doing on your computer with a surprised look in your blue eyes.

11

Dear Sasha,

We had never been in bed, just the two of us, except once when George had to leave for one night on some business, and we all knew that something was going to happen between us no matter how much we were planning to drink ourselves into oblivion. Our going to bed together and the ensuing sexual interaction was rather simple, like that of partners who have lived together for a long while. There was no flirting or burning looks or hot breaths or sexy comments about this part of the body or the other; there was just plain undressing, lying down and a quick petting before I felt you inside me and had to bite into your shoulder so that I did not scare the neighbours into calling the police or an ambulance. You were so very gentle and so very, very loving. And your every touch would give me the most tremendous pleasure.

But most nights, it was the three of us together. And most days, it was the three of us together around the kitchen table.

Our lives seemed to revolve around the kitchen table. Everybody was drawn to the cooker and the kettle and the toaster. I was amazed at all the extra space that went unused in the flats and houses we lived in. All those living rooms and dining rooms and family rooms and even conservatories, although housing some furniture, were usually left uninhabited. And however small the kitchen was, if we were able to fit the table in it, we would find a place for the three stools. The three laptops, three mugs, and an occasional glass of wine and a small cheese plate just had to somehow fit in as well. The kitchen – it doesn't matter the season or the weather – is always the home's womb, and I wonder why pechkas – the stove of your childhood you told me so much about, dear Sasha, with an oven on the bottom and a bunk-style sleeping space on top – are no longer a popular alternative to modern home architecture. If I were to design my perfect house, it would be one big kitchen, really, with a pechka as the centrepiece and a large, rectangular, rustic wooden table with benches as the other main furnishings. But unfortunately, we have to live in fairly modern flats due to the fact that we do enjoy the civilisation that big cities offer us, and no matter how comfy the home is, a cup of coffee with brioche does lift one's spirits every time. And I haven't noticed much of these being offered in local English villages.

12

Dear Sasha,

If you were to meet a Western gay man who was in the closet about his sexual orientation, you would probably have very different questions to ask him from what I asked you, dear Sasha, in the months following our first meeting. There were nights when I was so full of questions that I was bursting, but I had to wait for some time, until all of us felt comfortable with one another, to utter the first one over vodka shots and fried potatoes.

'Sasha, were you ever in love with a woman?'

Now, you would think this is the silliest question, and you responded to me with the very clever 'I was once in love with a car' comeback. 'Cried my eyes out when I had to get rid of it.'

You were so very careful with what you gave away. You measured your every response. You preferred to be quiet when the question seemed too intrusive. Sometimes a few vodka shots were not enough to get you talking, but when you did talk, you told stories I never thought I would hear or read about. These were stories of love – unrequited or reciprocated – and stories of lust. Both sets of stories fascinated me greatly, each in its own way. Sasha in love broke my heart. Sasha in lust turned me on. The ones I carefully avoided were the ones about you and other women, dear Sasha, as these made me feel very conflicted, including the stories about your family life.

On many occasions when you had to fly home, I knew exactly where you were going to stay – your family house, which your elderly parents shared with your wife. And what I knew very well was that you did feel some kind of affection for the woman you had once lived with. Although you did end up sleeping with George on your wedding night, ignoring your young bride after the reception, you then managed to cohabit with that woman for some time. And although I never felt jealous about you and your male conquests, dear Sasha, I did secretly get a nagging pain every time I thought about your other women. Of course you had sex with other women. Trying to prove something to yourself, probably, dear Sasha? To your straight friends? Your parents? This was the reason, I guess. And then that marriage. So rational a decision for a gay man of the time and place.

13

Dear Sasha,

I once told you that if I were to marry you, you wouldn't have to hide from me your relationships with other men, and you wouldn't have to lie to me ever. Quite the contrary, you would be able to go on a date and then tell me all the juicy details about it later on, and then we would both laugh and cry together and fall asleep cuddling in bed. I remember you said that I was being silly, and of course, I wouldn't have been happy about you announcing at dinner that you were about to go off for the night. So I turned around and told you that of course I wouldn't mind, as long as you put the kids to bed first and washed up the dishes and tidied up the kitchen and then kissed me goodnight and told me a story about your first love and then kissed me again and again and again. By that point, we were both laughing hysterically and woke up the cat, who glared at us with the nonchalant look of an animal who had been disturbed needlessly. We both love cats.

14

Dear Sasha,

I loved you. I don't think you loved me back. Not in that sort of way. In a friend sort of way, but not in an 'I would give everything just to see you smile' sort of way. The sort of way in which you loved George so many years ago. Remember, you told me that you knew back in your teens that those kinds of feelings were not reciprocated by most boys, and George in particular. You knew, and you couldn't help it. You told me that on one February night, you couldn't sleep, and you stormed out of your dorm at the back of the old brick building of the university's living quarters, trying to calm yourself by breathing in freezing air in deep gulps. You were sobbing; you were bashing your head on the brick wall the colour of rusted iron again and again. A young man of twenty, in love with another young man, in a society and in times in which such love was not merely looked down upon or laughed at, but prosecuted. Article 121 of the Criminal Code. Up to five years of hard labour.

15

Dear Sasha,

The other day, we all walked down to a local cafe. The pedestrian walk was wide enough for all three of us, and you grabbed my hand, as you often did. I grabbed George's, and then I caught a strange look from a middle-aged lady who was walking towards us, and I quickly let George's hand go. Whatever went through the mind of that woman, she might have thought about what she had seen for another minute or two, or the sight might have struck her such that she carried the visual with her well into the afternoon and into the tea rendezvous with her girlfriend or into the late-dinner chat with her husband.

The three of us rarely got 'the look' unless we were watched all the way through a meal by a diner at a table nearby. Then he or she might have noticed that I would hug you, dear Sasha, and place a peck on your cheek when you would say something sweet halfway through the meal, and then kiss George on the lips when he made a witty comment about the peculiar name of my pudding – that is, spotted dick. Whatever people gathered from such displays of my affection towards both men, I really could not guess, although I saw some of them widen their eyes or even trip on the way to their tables, but then, these were Brits, who were very much in control of their facial features and kept their emotions very deep inside themselves.

16

Dear Sasha,

You sometimes drank just a bit more than you should have. And you got teary once in a while. I was then ready with tissues, kind words and a shoulder to cry on. You had a few reasons to be depressed. You found out that you were gay very early, around the age of thirteen or so. You had a good childhood friend, a neighbour. Although your sexual attraction to Peter did surprise him early on, it did not stop him from allowing you to experiment on his body. Peter thus became your first sexual partner. Surprisingly, your friendship survived the experiment, and Peter, happily married now for many years and a father of three, although no longer an intimate partner, does consider himself a lifelong confidant.

The second friend, acquired sometime after your graduation from university, was a proper homosexual man, but just like you, he did not have much choice but to keep his desires in the closet and marry a woman at about the same time you were forced into a similar marriage. You two remained faithful to each other for years, first seeing each other often and then managing to travel back and forth every few months and writing and phoning each other regularly. The rest of your sexual partners – and there were many – were all short-term affairs; some were as quick as one-night stands, others lasting a week or two.

At which point your wife found out about your homosexual adventures, and whether she knew about them at all, remains a rather delicate subject. You claimed that there was no way a woman could not sense that kind of thing, but there was always a doubt in my mind that she understood the subject of sexuality well enough, as some women were brought up in very repressed environments in your part of the world. They were barely familiar with heterosexual sexuality, let alone with anything that went beyond the traditional relationship between the sexes. Your wife believed you to be a very reserved person, the kind you would see going out into the sunrise with a plough or a sickle and a faithful dog by his boots, and the kind who would come back home so very tired that he would greet his wife with a few dry words of encouragement about her daily housework, eat his dinner in silence, drink half a bottle of vodka, and fall asleep instantly once his head hit the pillow. However often you and your wife had sex and what kind of sex it was – whether your wife, having been raised in the rather sex-averse environment of the times, ever questioned the way inter-course was handled – I will never know. There were many families like yours. Sometimes these families were even more stable and long-lasting than many heterosexual families. I very much suspect that some of my friends' marriages are much more turbulent than that of you and your wife, dear Sasha.

17

Dear Sasha,

Divorces are infrequent in the undeveloped world. Sexual issues are rarely addressed, if at all. The financial issues are the ones of concern, not the emotional. Emotions are the prerogative of the spoiled inhabitants of the developed world. When we have climbed the needs ladder all the way from worrying about having a roof over our heads and food and water in abundance to feeling secure about social needs, only then do we embark on questioning such things as sexual and emotional intimacy and other fancy subjects of self-esteem, creativity, prejudice, or lack of it, and so on.

Love and belonging, although wanted by all humans no matter how rich or poor, is interpreted somewhat differently by different cultures in different parts of the world. To you or me, love could mean intimate conversations with a partner about how we feel about one another, with frequent private or public displays of affection. To your wife, dear Sasha, this could mean that her husband provides for her financially and phones home regularly to enquire about her health and that of her parents.

Whether or not the word love was ever used between the two of you remains unclear. I tried not to interrogate you much about your marriage. Your emotional intimacy with your wife was clearly non-existent. Your physical relationship with her did produce an infrequent quick ache in my heart when I heard her voice during your Skype conversations. And a couple of times, I felt completely broken when you travelled back home, and I felt so intensely that you disconnected from me and reconnected to your other world, to your extended family, all gathering together at the dinner table thousands of miles away from ours. I did not have that family connection with you, dear Sasha, so simple and so overwhelmingly recognised by society no matter the lack or presence of emotional intimacy. I was not your wife. Your relationship with me was one that would be scrutinised and looked down upon even by the most liberal members of our society. Were we lovers, dear Sasha, you and I? Were we very close friends? Who were we? And who were you, dear Sasha?

18

Dear Sasha,

You asked me once, when your sobbing woke me up at three in the morning after we had all managed to go to bed an hour earlier, who you were – gay, straight or bi? You desired a man's body; you fell in love with men. You had many times. At the same time, you had managed to marry a woman and live with her for almost a quarter of a century. While it is so easy to explain all the above as society's coercion of you into obedience, it is much more difficult to deal with the emotional side of things.

I think what you also found difficult to deal with, dear Sasha, was understanding your emotional and even occasional sexual attraction to me, a woman – a very boyish, jeans-and-trainers-wearing woman who never had any trace of makeup on her face, but nevertheless, a woman – with all the female bits and pieces that homosexual men have no need for. I do not attempt to imply that you were chasing me around the house or trying to woo me over romantic dinners, like I was so used to heterosexual men doing. And often our sexual intercourse was probably very similar to that of you and your wife, with quick penetrations and quick relief, but once in a while, after some sleepless nights with never-ending conversations about life's meaning, I saw a different you, dear Sasha. Your eyes would be fixed on mine; you would pull me towards you with the strength and desire of any straight man. You were a wonderful kisser, and in moments like these, we would kiss for eternity. And having these moments, however rare they were, was the greatest gift of all. In bed on these nights, you would be different; whether I was a woman and you were a man and which sexual orientation and which sexual subgroup we belonged to would be unclear, as we would just be lovers, and our bodies would connect and respond to one another. Who were we? What were we?

19

Dear Sasha,

I am frequently forgetting about George in these letters. In my conquest for you and your heart and body, George became more of my confidant, just like I was his in our many philosophical discussions about his relationship with you. Of course, you had feelings for George that went back a quarter of a century earlier, and George did have an advantage over me: he had the right bits. I was somehow never jealous. By default, you, dear Sasha, would be physically more attracted to George, and that was very apparent on a daily basis. Most of the time, at least, you would hug and kiss George whenever the two of you were in proximity to each other, and the situation would be favourable. However, most nights, if we did end up in bed, we ended up in bed all together. I would always initiate the intimate contact. I could never wait until the whole bottle of wine had been emptied, and you, dear Sasha, would end up singing a few songs while doing some simple guitar chords. At some point during the night, after the umpteenth cigarette, I would kiss your neck while we chatted on the balcony. I would kiss you just below the ear, knowing all your most sensitive spots, and would go down to your shoulder, gently lifting the collar of your shirt. I would go under the collarbone and stroke your chest lightly with my lips and the tip of my nose and my fingers while unbuttoning your shirt. You would freeze, dear Sasha. You could never resist whatever I was doing. We would go back indoors quickly and shut the balcony door, as you were afraid to be noticed by neighbours or passersby. You had this fear of public displays of affection, forgetting that it was safe here in the West, even if you were to do it with another man on our balcony in plain view of the entire neighbourhood. This would get some kind of attention, of course, but heterosexual couples making love in public were simply ignored altogether.

Once we were inside the flat, I would work my fingers and my lips down your torso and all the way down to your waist. I would by then be on my knees, unbuttoning your jeans and working magic with my tongue while stroking your back with my fingers. Once I learned how to please a man back in my early teens, I took the art of oral sex quite seriously and was told on quite a few occasions that I was really good at it. I would stroke your testicles and your penis with the tip of my nose and just slightly touch the head of your penis with my lips and the tip of my tongue. I would

40

then kiss your inner thighs gently, the left one and then the right. I would return back to the groin area and take hold of the base of your penis with my fingers while slowly kissing the tip of it, the small meatus on top of the penis's head, and then carefully take the whole head in my mouth, working my tongue on the little bridle and then returning again to the meatus opening and gently sticking my tongue inside it.

You, by then, would moan and pull me by my shoulders towards the bedroom, as you always preferred to indulge in oral pleasures while lying down. I would get myself comfortable on my knees and elbows while you would just close your eyes and lie back motionless on the bed. I knew then that you were all mine, and I would take the rest of the fondling and caressing as slowly as I could until I drove you completely mad. I would alternate between sucking on just the head of your penis to completely taking it in my mouth, the fingers of one hand firmly on the base and the fingers of the other hand remembering the piano lessons of my youth. I would imagine a keyboard and would slowly run my fingers up and down your back or your chest or your buttocks. Usually I would get so aroused by the noises that you made and by the way you grabbed my shoulders that I would be completely wet.

I would wait until I felt that you could hold no longer and would abruptly stop my oral exercises. I would then push myself forward, take your penis and slide it inside me.

You were big. I, however, by then wouldn't care much, as I would be way too aroused for any sensation except complete bliss. I would slowly lower myself all the way until my buttocks could feel your thighs and testicles.

You would never open your eyes during our lovemaking. I think I saw you open your eyes once only. And then you looked at me with complete bemusement, as if you did not recognise me at all. I would generally be on top, sometimes persuading you to go on your side and enter me from behind, pulling my body against yours. I would bite your forearm, feeling how your biceps rolled under my neck and my cheek. I would grip the end of the bed to find some stability, and I would feel your body behind me, lightly touching me and then pulling away. We would go on like this for what seemed like hours, although in reality it would only be minutes. You would bite my ear just before coming. I would feel your body stiffen and then relax, and I would lie like that, trying to retain your smell and the sensation of your body against mine. I would be so, so scared at times that every time you and I made love, it might be our last, dear Sasha.

20

Dear Sasha,

Once in a while, I witnessed you and George making out. The first time, you got carried away, remember, and forgot all about me? The spectacle was something I hadn't expected to react so strongly to. I became very aroused. I remember reading about men being aroused by two lesbians making out. However, I have never heard of females having a similar reaction to watching two men having sex. I assume I haven't been reading the right female magazines.

When I first saw you and George moving in bed, I think I forgot to breathe I was so still. I probably became almost invisible too. Then you glanced up and almost fell out of bed from what I believe was the sudden shock of seeing me in the same room. I must have looked shocked myself. I remember I realised that I had to say something – and say something quickly. I couldn't just leave the room. 'This is so beautiful,' I repeated a few times, almost under my breath. My throat was dry.

You and George, of course, stopped the action altogether. I slipped in between you and started kissing you and George, taking turns, inflicting hot, dry kisses on both of your faces and necks. I remember you taking hold of my hands and pushing me against the bed and entering me almost forcefully and angrily, moving inside me rapidly with the roughness of a man who just had to have his way and had to have it right at that moment. You came quickly, then got out of bed and left the room instantly as George and I continued where you had left off, although much more gently. I loved having both of you to myself.

21

Dear Sasha,

We had our fights, of course. Do you remember? You would turn in early some nights, dear Sasha. This would happen without warning. You would not show any signs of distress the whole day, but then sometime towards dinnertime, I would notice some strain in the way you responded to things, a spoon falling on the floor, my question about whether you were all right, my suggestion to watch a film. I would start to get nervous, as it always pained me to watch you feeling low. I would feel a sense of failure, somehow responsible for your bad mood, or rather, for not making you happier. I could never see these moods coming. You would excuse yourself from the table at dinner even if you had cooked and looked quite happy in the process. You would say that you needed to take an early shower and would never come out of your bedroom. When, an hour later, I would gently knock and take a peek inside the room,

I would see you fast asleep, your snoring getting louder and louder as the evening progressed.

On nights like this, I would get so very miserable that even if George, sensing my disappointment, offered to go for a walk or a short drive – or proposed any other entertainment, for that matter – I would refuse. Somehow things would stop mattering, as I could not imagine getting any pleasure from these simple activities. You would be missing from all of them, dear Sasha. And the whole night and my whole life would stop making sense.

I once sneaked into your bed when you were either sleeping already or about to fall asleep or just pretending that you were asleep so that you could be left alone. That didn't work out well at all. You got so very cross with me, jumped up and stormed out of the room. Only much later did I figure out that it was not me you wanted in your bed on those nights. It was not even George. You wanted to be there alone with your thoughts and memories. A half-naked woman was usually not part of either.

22

Dear Sasha,

Languages are the thing that got both you and George into the university's languages department and onto each other's path. You used to like telling the story over and over again about the first time you two saw each other.

It was your third year in the university, and George's first exchange visit to the former USSR. George was walking along the corridor, looking for a language lab, and figuring you definitely looked older than the freshers – and thus knew the university well – he asked you for directions. The two of you struck up a conversation. Languages and the cultures these languages define were and still are your main passion. You and George could converse in French or German for hours, depending on the topic.

I can't speak either. I did take up French at some point at university, but that was a while ago, and I did end up understanding about a quarter of what was being said between the two of you. Most of it I was guessing once I could figure out the topic of conversation. With German, I couldn't understand anything at all; I would guess an occasional word, but I would be in the dark about the theme discussed. However, I did love the sound of both languages, and I could just listen to you two talk, dear Sasha; it didn't matter which language was involved. However, I do have a weakness for French. French films were something I loved watching with both of you. I asked for subtitles. This narrowed the choice, but there was still plenty to watch, my ears enjoying the sound of the language spoken by either women or men. With German, I preferred the women's version of the language, which made this harsh tongue a bit softer. I would turn my head between you and George, watching how your lips were moving, not so much trying to understand what was being said as enjoying your articulation and the music of either language.

We would dream of living in either country, remember? We would talk about living in a village, far from civilisation, to have privacy and escape from the world. The next day, we would dream of living in the centre of Bordeaux or Paris or Marseille, having excellent access to pain au chocolat and coffee and baguettes stuffed with chicken salad or sausages and veggies. German bread and yogurts were remembered fondly from previous trips. So German villages would be favoured over French, although we all wouldn't stop salivating when remembering a recent stay at a French goat farm, where the lady of the house rolled soft cheese in different kinds of herbs, and the delivery boy from the bakery in the nearby town stopped every morning with freshly baked bread.

We would sleep late usually, remember? George would respond to the baker's car horn, jump out of bed and run down the narrow staircase from the bedrooms to the front door to get the goodies, usually leaving them on the kitchen table and climbing back into bed for another hour or two. We then took turns making coffee, or I would make all three, although you were never happy with the way I made yours. Too much honey or sugar. Too little milk. Croissants would be eaten, and we would walk to the people at the farmhouse and collect a tall jar of fresh goat's milk and a few rolls of cheese. These would last until evening, when we were ready to get the duck eggs out of the fridge for an omelette, accompanied by a bottle of wine from the owner's wine cellar.

The house was one of the barns refurbished into guest accommodation and belonging to the estate of a retired ambassador. His photographs with world-famous political leaders adorned the walls. We never saw him personally, as his estate manager dealt with short-term lettings, but we did get a welcome letter from him and his wife, warning us that they expected to find everything – art, furniture and presumably wine – in the same order they had left it in for us.

We honestly did not touch any of the art. It was the wine we couldn't resist. George justified this by the fact that we could not get a proper internet connection where one was clearly advertised in the rental ad. As we couldn't get online, what were we to do with our free time? Drink wine, of course. And take long walks in the woods, trying to figure out which oak tree King Louis – whichever his regnal number – had been resting under when he had gone out hunting in this part of France, as the oak tree was also mentioned in the ad.

On one of our car rides, we passed a house that was surrounded by old pieces of furniture and bric-a-brac sitting on the dried, yellowed grass, on two cracked benches and hanging on the fence. I love all things vintage and antique, finding joy in old things that could hardly have served much purpose back when they were used, let alone now. We stopped the car, glanced around the front garden and then decided to try what looked like the main door, which creaked into a cellar-cold hall where the sun probably hadn't even touched a windowsill for a couple of centuries. Out of the gloom, a man staggered, carrying a fierce smell of naphthalene and whisky-charged breath. He stroked his holey, antiquated sweater and pointed lazily to a far-off room in the shadows. Remember, dear Sasha?

'Do you know,' he sang beautifully in his drunken French, 'Louis XVI was captured here while fleeing revolutionary Paris?' His voice echoed in the narrow corridors. Well, this was my enhanced and refined translation, or at least what I understood from a speech he gave you and George once he realised the two of you spoke the language.

The shabby man smelling of liquor was probably less than articulate in his still beautifully musical, drunken French, but all three of you managed to get some discussion going about a few most unusual items on the lot, and then you explained to me, dear Sasha, that the old house was a former postal office and that the man's story was probably very true, as, from what you had read a long time ago in one of the history books, Louis XVI was taken to the Tuileries Palace in 1789, from which he tried to flee two years later. On the journey to escape, the king stopped in Sainte-Menehould, the very place we were passing through, he was identified by the local postmaster, who recognised the king's face from a portrait and alerted the town authorities of his presence. It looked like his old post office had been turned into a house and sold to its present occupant, who smelled of whisky. The king was apprehended in Varennes, the small town from which our baker brought us croissants every morning. I remember being quite taken aback by the story and then walking through the rooms of the former post office once more and touching the heavy beams with the curiosity of a person who had missed all the revolutions that had happened in the world in the past few centuries, except for the ones that were taking place inside her.

23

Dear Sasha,

Back in London, having barely made it to the ferry in Calais, because our tyre burst halfway between Sainte-Menehould and the port, we all returned to the flat exhausted. I stumbled through, as I had been behind the wheel for most of the journey – I could never trust either you or George to drive anywhere beyond the M25. It's not that you and George can't drive, but I do it better, and I get less carsick when I am in the driver's seat.

Our flat had a very unusual smell. None of my previous homes had smelled that way; it is hard to describe, but it used to remind me somewhat of fried potatoes with onions – which could be easily explained by the fact that the flat was right on top of a pub. The pub on the ground floor and the three storeys of flats, including ours on top, were originally built in 1830s and have since been restored and remodelled many times, the latest improvement being the floor. The improvement before that was probably the piping, which I think was messed up somehow, as the water was never consistently either hot or cold, no matter what time of day someone turned on the tap or the shower and no matter how careful we were of not running the washing machine or the dishwasher at the same time.

The street itself, King's Road, is one of the most famous in London and was named so after King Charles II, as it was once apparently his private road from Westminster to Fulham, and he never travelled through without paying a visit to his mistress, Nell Gwyn – at least, that's what the elderly pub owner told everyone who settled down for a drink at the bar. At the time of King Charles II, the road was reported to have been a narrow rural path that passed through swamps haunted by robbers but nevertheless served as the main access from Westminster to one of the main Thames crossings. It is hard to imagine the swamps or the robbers nowadays. The widened and many times rebuilt King's Road now passes through many restaurants – mainly French and Italian, according to the names – and small shops selling everything from South American–inspired clothing to hardwood flooring and furniture. My favourites were the local charity shops, which – thanks to the well-to-do residents of the area – had a good selection of both cashmere sweaters and books, and you, dear Sasha, put more than one of these antique treasures and smelly torn jackets aside and smiled at me like a parent would smile at a child running through the front door with a dead frog or a half-broken toy found on the kerb.

24

Dear Sasha,

The days were always punctuated by your cigarette breaks. The first one came with a cup of black coffee in the morning. The last one, after your nightly shower. There were dozens in between. If there was any order in spacing them, it was a mystery to me. Whether it was your body clock telling you when to pick one from the pack, just like tea drinkers know when it is time for another cup, I am not sure. But then I do press the kettle button a few times a day, so why wouldn't anyone else want to do something many times over, like light a cigarette?

25

Dear Sasha,

To get you to do anything of an amorous nature before the dark fell was impossible. For some people, daylight just kills the mystery of romance. The preparations were allowed, though. The big dinners, for example, which were usually a good indication that you were in the mood for love. Planning for these could start quite early in the day, as they were usually in themselves quite sensual. The washing, the slicing, the mixing, the addition of assorted spices, the handling of pots and pans of various sizes, the turning on of the oven and the hobs, the lining up of the various knives on the multitude of wooden slicing and chopping boards …

I was allowed to participate. George was not. He was kicked out of the kitchen on many occasions and had to stay at least a few feet away for being too noisy about what was cooked and how, for giving annoying suggestions and for being a 'pain in everybody's behind'.

It's not enough, apparently, to have chemistry in the bedroom. The kitchen chemistry is as important as the one in the living room, the one in the library or office – assuming your flat has one or the other – and the one in the house generally, as some people just cannot cohabit no matter how witty they find each other's conversations and how pleasant the company and how sexually charged the experience when they meet on neutral territory. I do not think chemistry is something that can be learned over time. Rather, it is adjusted a little if the initial chemistry is there. If you can cook dinner together without getting on each other's nerves, you can live together happily for many years – pardon me, months, many months making a year, and maybe some more. You, dear Sasha, and I have managed to make dinners in many kitchens around the world, even in tiny little kitchenettes in studios, with nothing more than an electric two-hob stove, one old frying pan and a dull knife.

The recipes were discussed right after breakfast, and ingredients were shopped for around lunchtime, and that was when a quick bite of a burger or its regional alternative of a stuffed flatbread, falafel or a packed sandwich was grabbed on the way between the shops. The table was set at sunset, and dinners were accompanied by just the right amount of alcohol, the amount that was to be consumed during the meal and the after-dinner entertainment of guitar playing and singing or listening to original versions on YouTube.

And then there were desserts, also accompanied by alcohol, and then a cigarette break by the window or on the porch or on the balcony, depending on what was available, and only then was I allowed the first move leading up to the bedroom – although a kiss on the neck, a hug, and a peck on the cheek were all possible upon completion of the cooking stage.

26

Dear Sasha,

You were raised in a place and time in which public displays of affection were looked down upon, even between married people. All kissing and lovemaking were to be done in the privacy of one's bedroom, not even to be professed around the children or the close relatives of the couple. Any gesture could apparently be considered an inappropriate display of affection, even as asexual in nature as holding hands, although that was the only one you did approve of in public. However, any other kind of touching, kissing or hugging was a no-no, even if it was a goodbye scene at the airport and the parties involved were parting for eternity.

As I had lived most of my life in the West, I was used to seeing people perform overt gestures to signify sexual or romantic liking and not feeling that there was anything wrong with it. As we travelled eastward, you, dear Sasha, found yourself more at home with the local ordinances regarding the taboo on open-mouth kissing and intense fondling in public arenas. Coming from a less permissive culture, you, of course, not only could not imagine pulling me close in the middle of the supermarket but were barely even receptive to any kind of joke or comment that related to close relationships between men and women – or men and men, for that matter.

27

Dear Sasha,

Back in the kitchen, where our shoulders rubbed more often than not, as our kitchens were all rather small, once the sun had set and the need for artificial light had arisen, you would mellow down and slowly relax, as you were a night animal. Your eyes would light up at the sight of the dining table filling with plates and cups and wine glasses, and you would grab a slice of bread from the breadbasket on the way to light your last cigarette before sitting down for the meal. A few minutes later, you would reappear with a half-empty beer bottle and a visibly lighter mood. The last preparations over, George would then be located and gently pulled away from his laptop or his magazine or his book. The meal then would begin with hors d'oeuvres and wine accompanied by toast after toast on topics of health, prosperity and other related matters.

The main course would be eaten next, interrupted by yet another cigarette break; this time, all three of us would come out for a smoke and a pleasant conversation under the moon and stars, and this would be the time that I would get my share of a shoulder massage or a gentle kiss or an even more passionate embrace from you, dear Sasha. The memories would start flowing, the stories about the distant and not-so-distant past would be told by each of us taking turns, laughing, switching languages depending on the nationality of the main characters of the narrative or location of the tale. We would also try to use a language not spoken in the area, for fear that our less-than-innocent conversations would be overheard by the neighbours. To the latter, the trio on the balcony would just be friends having a good laugh. Which we were. The fact that this trio would later end up in bed, doing what was usually the scenario for two participants of the same or opposite sex, had so far escaped every neighbour we'd ever had, or at least they kept it to themselves once they had found out. Even the closest of our friends and relatives seemed to be ignorant of the nature of our relationship. To them, you, dear Sasha, were a school friend who came to visit.

28

Dear Sasha,

We were sitting on a bench covered with splashes of falafel sauce, one of the benches where the famous Falafellow falafels were consumed by hungry tourists and locals after queuing for at least half an hour outside the tiny shop. All three of us were leaning over our lunches, trying not to splatter the sauce on our jeans and trainers, the taste of yogurt mixed with lemon zest and the smell of coriander, parsley and cumin in the air making us ravenous. We had almost inhaled our falafels, completely ignoring a number of beggars who had constantly harassed the queuing crowd for change and had only agreed to give everyone a break once the chef had slowed them down with some falafels and a few cans of Coca-Cola. Part of the Acropolis was visible from the street leading to the ruins via souvenir stalls and a bric-a-brac bazaar. The April sun was bearable; it was the perfect time to come to the southern parts of the world if you wanted to enjoy sightseeing rather than endure it.

I performed the Hollywood cliché move of dabbing a bit of sauce from your cheek, dear Sasha. You sprang backwards, having not expected my gesture, and I suddenly got moody. It must just have been my hormones playing a trick on me, and a few days earlier, I wouldn't have reacted that way. I would have realised that we were outside, in plain view of hundreds, and of course, you wouldn't want to be touched or loved or even stared at adoringly in such surroundings. But there were some days when, knowing all that, I still ached for the minuscule signs of affection from you that I thought I properly deserved, having spent the better part of the previous night loving you.

George, the most cold-blooded member of our trio, was content to stride through the entire city, breaking for snacks without the need for physical connection or the reassurance of continuous affection that I always longed for. You, dear Sasha, were raised to restrain yourself from any such displays, but I just wanted to be swept off my feet in the middle of our stroll through the most tourist-filled promenade and just be smooched all over, tightly hugged and then gazed at adoringly. And it seemed like I would never have it my way with any of the men in my life.

You didn't like my moody spells just as much as I was absolutely horrified by yours. Ours rarely coincided, but they seemed to feed one another, and as moody spells usually go, ours were contagious. That meant that if I were to spend the better part of that Athens afternoon making it really obvious that I was underloved, then you, dear Sasha, would get your sullen spell around dinnertime or even sometime later than that, which was far worse. An early shower and a double dose of alcohol and cigarettes accompanied by some terse Skype or Facebook chatting would communicate to the rest of us that you were to be left alone to dwell on your sorrowful past. Which, of course, you were allowed to do. All of us were. But it just so happened that we could not always match our humours and tempers. So when one sulked, the rest suffered. These things, of course, happen in regular two-partner couples just as well. It's just when there are three people involved, things get even more complicated.

29

Dear Sasha,

You made love with your eyes closed. Whether you considered lovemaking an embarrassing experience or whether you were trying to imagine someone else in my or George's place remained a mystery. I am guessing a bit of both. You also thought that talking during sex had no use whatsoever. One is supposed to guess, infer – imagine, maybe – interpret one's partner's thoughts and grimaces and utterances to the best of one's abilities. One is not to name the body parts. This is what you and your fellow citizens in sexually repressed cultures were unfortunately brought up to believe sex was all about. The recent injection of the Western, all-uninhibited culture into the one you, dear Sasha, were brought up in did very little, as one is more influenced by such things during one's youth, and of course, by the time the USSR's Iron Curtain was lifted, you were an adult. With maturity comes a certain rigidity of mind.

During moments of passion, you would remain very calm and composed. I have seen you lose yourself only twice. Once was when the three of us were in bed together. It only lasted half a minute or so. I held my breath and watched how you lightly placed a kiss on George's shoulder while he was still asleep. It was early morning. None of us were early birds, really. That meant waking up side by side did not always bring out the best in anyone.

That particular morning, though, the sun was quite determined to get everyone on their feet, as not even the curtain – dark, chequered and designed to withstand the brightest of rays – could defend our eyes from the annoying light. It was already past nine, according to our wall clock, which had not been moved forward to reflect the summer time, and somehow we had just got used to adding one hour to the time indicated on its face. I was sitting on the edge of the bed, pulling my sweatshirt on and trying to remember where I had abandoned my glasses the night before, when I heard the bedsprings make the clanking noise of a trampoline at the moment of landing after a particularly long and pleasant jump.

You, dear Sasha, and I took turns sleeping in the middle – never George, for some reason. I preferred the warmth of two bodies on both sides of me for the simple reason of always being the 'froggy' in the trio, having cold hands and feet and generally feeling the temperature fluctuations more acutely. However, that night, you, dear Sasha, had ended up sleeping in the middle.

Thus, as I turned my head to see what was going on, I became a witness to one of those rare moments in which you actually had your eyes open and were intensely eyeing George's half-naked torso, our blanket covering only the bottom of his stomach and thighs, leaving his chest, his lower legs, and his arms all bare and lit up by the sun. You touched George's shoulder with your lips, then slowly moved your mouth to his upper arm, along his bicep, down to the elbow and then stopped briefly to lift yourself on one arm and lower your mouth to George's neck. You moved your lips further, barely touching George's skin, rather tickling than kissing. Then you moved from his neck to his chest, to one of his nipples, circling it, and moved down to his belly button, to his lower stomach and then the edge of his pubic hair.

George started grimacing, slowly being woken up by the foreplay – or for that matter, the whole act, really, as I found it rather complicated separating the parts of the sexual act into the 'getting into it', 'it' and 'after it'. For all I knew, what I had just witnessed was the whole 'it'.

I don't think you, dear Sasha, meant to go any further with your burst of morning tenderness, especially when you became aware of my presence for a moment. Although I did hold my breath, as I mentioned, I might have been so transfixed by what I was witnessing that I hadn't noticed how I scrunched the edge of the blanket in my fist and some-how made it move. You glanced up at me. I looked straight into your eyes, suddenly so different in shade and shape, with the geometry of lines around them repositioning and making them look so much more beautiful, making you into a different person, really, the one I have so far glimpsed only a handful of times. You smiled at me. Then your eyes slowly returned back to the shade and shape I was used to. I climbed back onto the bed, lightly kissed your shoulders, quickly got up again and ran into the kitchen. For all I knew, dear Sasha, at that moment, you must have remembered your and George's youth, the times when it was just the two of you.

30

Dear Sasha,

Once there are three people in a relationship, there are times, of course, when you remember with fondness being part of a duo – or being single, for that matter. Just like after having a child, you are bound to stop in your tracks in the middle of rushing through Costco with a mocha and a take-away blueberry muffin wrapped in paper, single-handedly pushing a stroller with your screaming offspring, and suddenly realise that there were times when you could just sit there with your laptop and your muffin on a gleaming plate, picking up crumbs and a few lonely blueberries, contemplating the first hot sip of your coffee and the rest of your life. Those were the good times, of course, you reminisce, but your current life, with your cranky toddler and older, even crankier pre-teen, is even better. And so is the life George and I share – at times so simple when it was just the two of us in the relationship, but much, much, much more complete with you, dear Sasha, in it. At times, though, it seemed to be just a bit too much. But we got through it for a good stretch of time.

31

Dear Sasha,

'The designated emergency exit for this relationship is the door opposite the kitchen.'

I woke up at five that morning. The outside of the square-netted window was white painted with fog. I was in bed alone. My period had started the day before. I was not in a good mood, to say the least, so I had shut the door in your faces after delivering a couple of lines most women regret once their hormones are back to normal. I remember wrapping myself in a duvet like a mummy and falling asleep almost immediately. However, at five in the morning, I struggled out of bed and clumsily ventured out of the bedroom and into the living room to find George dozing at the computer desk, his head resting on his hands, and you, dear Sasha, fast asleep on the couch with the Marina Tsvetaeva memoir on your lap. You two, poor men, had been camping in the living room since the night before. Your blonde hair, dear Sasha, was covering your forehead; the palm of your hand, your eyes, as if to shield you from intense light. I could see just your mouth. Lips parted. Yours were thin lips always pressed together tightly as if guarded against saying something you would later regret. You are a silent type. Guessing what was going on inside your head from the way you stared at the morning fog, from the way you ate, smoked and drank or from what you were reading became my daily game.

On the way back from the bathroom, I carefully picked up the book from your lap. Shivering, I decided to steal it and investigate it back under the thick duvet. Some of the lines were highlighted with the yellow marker that had mysteriously disappeared from my desk drawer a few days before:

'If you love two people at the same time, you love none!' But excuse me – if I love N. and I love Heinrich Heine, you cannot say that I do not love the former. So one could love the dead and the alive one at the same time. However, just imagine if Heinrich Heine came back to life and theoretically at any moment could enter the room. I am still the same person. Heinrich Heine is still the same. The only difference is that he could enter the room.

Verdict: feeling love toward two people simultaneously, when either of them could enter the room at any time, is impossible. In order for my feelings for both people to be real, it is absolutely necessary for one of these people to be born a hundred years before me or not to be born at all (for example, a portrait, a poem). Not always a satisfiable condition.

It was followed by this:

I have no ranking order in my feelings. I am like a child that way.

And this:

Better to lose someone with your whole self than to keep him with a small part of self.

My thoughts upon shutting the book: Tsvetaeva is worth rereading once again, and my suspicion that you, dear Sasha, write poetry must have been correct all along.

32

Dear Sasha,

I left a plastic timer too close to the stove once. You would think they would design them to withstand heat. The apple-stuffed chicken in a bath of vegetable broth was overcooked, the apples churned, the broth evaporated. The melted timer had failed to chime. It was my attempt at an interpretation of an American Thanksgiving meal, given it had been Thanksgiving the day before, and we had lived in the United States some years earlier, where those holidays mandated that any kind of fowl – predominantly turkey – be roasted and consumed while surrounded by family. Ours didn't work out, perhaps because none of us were American, and the kitchen we had gathered in to mourn the chicken be-longed to a tiny London flat.

I took the incident rather badly, although both you, dear Sasha, and George offered to run to at least a dozen takea-way restaurants at the same time or order various American-inspired meals to be brought to us within a short period of time. I rejected all offers. I cried. I blamed you for turning the sound up too high while watching a television show, so loud that we could not possibly hear anything, including the melted timer's attempt at alerting us to the readiness of the meal. I blamed George's inattentiveness to my delicate hormonal condition by not replacing me at the stove and doing a better job of safeguarding the timer. I cried. I yelled. I slammed doors. First the kitchen's. Then the bathroom's. Then the bedroom's. I noticed the next morning, however, on my way to the bathroom, that the chicken, as overdone as it was, had all been consumed, with the carcass still sitting in the middle of the dinner table. Hungry men do not mind imperfections.

33

Dear Sasha,

You once told me that back in your youth, you used to fall asleep with the short-wave radio next to your pillow, trying to listen to programmes from the other side of the Iron Curtain. The airways were jammed by the governments in Communist countries during much of the Cold War, utilising all kinds of techniques to add extra noise to the same short waves that were used by the Western radio stations for their East-directed propaganda. The most common noises that the short-wave listeners in the Eastern Bloc heard were all kinds of sweep-through noises, pulsing noises, random Morse code messages and even interference from diesel generators.

Radio Free Europe, Radio Liberty, Voice of America, and the BBC World Service were the favourites of Soviet jammers and Soviet listeners alike, you told me. As these radio programmes were transmitted in more than one language, the jamming was usually only directed at the languages spoken in the Eastern Bloc, like Russian, Ukrainian, Latvian, Georgian and the like; thus, those who were lucky enough to be fluent in French, German or English, like you, were also lucky enough to often enjoy uninterrupted broadcasting of their favourite programmes.

Very often, music rather than any political anti-Communist-saturated news was what the listeners were after, but the blanket jamming order was imposed on most Western programming, so jazz became as political as it could never have been imagined to be by New Orleans street performers. Some handy radio lovers built homemade loop antennas. Some, like you, dear Sasha, and your clever mathematician friends, even came up with various formulas to calculate the times when particular jamming transmitters were temporarily off air due to maintenance.

In the late 1980s, when most Communist governments had stopped jamming, so disappeared the familiar Morse code and vacuum-cleaner-inspired wailing noises through which barely a few words spoken by the news broadcasters could be understood. And although everyone was celebrating the ability to listen to their favourite programmes with ease, the desire to tune in to the famous Radio Liberty or Voice of America slowly waned as all kinds of information became widely available and easily accessible through suddenly free and sensation-hungry media. You told us, dear

Sasha, that the familiar theme tunes of Radio Liberty's many programmes still play in your head today.

34

Dear Sasha,

Another favourite story from you and George was about meeting for the first time during George's 'Train of Friendship' visits to the small Ukrainian town of Gogol, right outside the capital of Kyiv, housing the Kyiv State Linguistic University. Both you and George were majoring in French and minoring in German. During the Cold War, it was a rather rare and important occasion for the university in the Communist Bloc to host Western students, who were rarely allowed to venture beyond the walls of campuses and were bussed around the capital followed by two police cars and a few KGB representatives making sure no inappropriate contact was made between the West and the East.

This official student visit started with the university president's long speech and the department directors' supporting shorter speeches in the larger lecture hall, with students from both sides of the border dozing off from boredom. It was mid-November. The heating was on full, and the double-glazed windows were filled up with clusters of cotton yellowing at the edges and littered with little black dots that turned out to be dead bugs upon your close inspection. These insects had made a fatal mistake in landing on the fibre chunks as the caretakers had been winterproofing the university windows a couple of weeks before and were now part of a window bug cemetery, which many students were staring at while listening to the monotonous voice of yet another person in a suit.

You all had a choice of blankly staring at the speaker, the dead bugs or the roof of the university's library, dusted with snow, lightly covering a few empty cigarette packs, a bottle of Coca-Cola and other miscellaneous rubbish. And that was when George overheard you and your friends whispering. One of the professors coughed angrily to intimidate the naughty students, making George turn his head in the direction of the cough and see you, dear Sasha, the boy whom he had bumped into earlier on the staircase. He stared at you momentarily and then turned to another fair-haired, blue-eyed young man sitting next to you and relaying something in an inaudible whisper. George felt someone's gentle elbow nudge, and a small piece of paper was stuffed into the right-side pocket of his blazer.

'The meeting is adjourned,' the loud voice of the speaker barked into the microphone, and the following rummaging and rustling of the couple of hundred students and professors alike, folding papers into bags and satchels, confirming their afternoon plans with each other, slowly dissolved into the overwhelming racket of youngsters' laughter, whistling, yelling and the other appropriate noises of any university hall.

George did not have a chance to examine the paper until an hour later, as he claimed, when the Westerners were all put in the buses for the afternoon city sightseeing tour. The note read:

La Bibliothèque de Lénine. Étagères des dictionnaires. 19.00.

And that is how it all began, with poor George shivering at the library for at least half an hour, as he had decided to come early and investigate its contents. The university's heating system hadn't been updated since the campus's 1943 overhaul, resulting from the German bomb leaving only the four walls standing and nothing much inside but the rubble of the grand staircase. The library was sparsely furnished with a couple of dozen bare desks, a multitude of bookshelves and a noticeboard covering a particularly blotchy and shabby piece of wall. A couple of massive electric typing machines with a stack of copy paper dwarfed all the other miscellaneous office supplies. Two coat stands in the corner of the room angrily pointed their naked wooden branches up at the ceiling. No one, however, wanted to part with their coats and scarves in this cold, including George, as he remembered. Winterproofed windows didn't help much, as the insulation had been long ago eaten through by famished rats, and one could stick a finger between the cracked white window frames of the library and the thinly painted, wide windowsills that George attempted to sit on but was shushed off by an elderly librarian. The old lady uttered something angrily that George, not being fluent in Ukrainian, could not understand at all, but the woman's gestures spoke clearly something in a way of 'You must be blind or stupid to not see the chairs in front of you – the windowsills are not for sitting on.'

35

Dear Sasha,

The chemical imbalance that comes with infatuation tends to be quite problematic for getting through everyday events, as it affects one's concentration, emotional balance, energy and memory. Succumbing to being in love is something that feels so natural when one is in one's early or late teens, and it ends up providing that young person with extraordinary entertainment – which, in the early 1970s, tended to be one of a few on offer, given that the internet and the multitude of gadgets available nowadays had not even been imagined back then. George became the object of your affections, dear Sasha, following your falling-out with one of your professors, who – after drowning the eighteen-year-old you in forty-plus years of memories almost nightly in the empty, poorly lit and barely heated department chair rooms – got back with his estranged wife, and your affair and your nightly meetings ceased. There were a couple of young men at the university who accepted your affection with a greater or lesser degree of accord, but none turned out to be as receptive as George.

The relationship took on a routine of its own since the library date after the two of you had gone through initial introductions. You met nightly in different classrooms or dorms or even TV lounges in social clubs, where your cigarettes produced just enough light to transform smoke-fogged rooms into magic caves where you both wanted to hide from the world to talk Adamo, Aznavour, Gainsbourg, Piaf, Balzac, Stendhal, Hugo, Flaubert and everybody and everything French. You compared and contrasted your childhoods, the Eastern and the Western. You wrote poems to each other; you read them out loud. You shared luke-warm chicken broth, sandwiches or stuffed crêpes from a nearby cafe.

36

Dear Sasha,

George told you that where he came from, bananas and French literature abounded, and he didn't have to queue to get either. You, dear Sasha, on the other hand, had to buy your favourite fruit while they were still green and then wrap them in old newspaper sheets and keep them in the wardrobe for another two weeks, waiting for them to ripen. You told George that the sound an unripe banana skin makes when it is torn from the fruit made you clench your teeth, and you couldn't help but peek in the cupboard a few times a day to check if the bananas' green colour was at all changing into yellow. The ready-to-eat colour was supposed to be deep yellow with brown spots, but you only had enough patience to let it get to light yellow, if yellow at all.

37

Dear Sasha,

You once told me that, as a child, you used to fall asleep tracing your fingers through the thick, dusty fur of a wall carpet, finding your path in a labyrinth of complex patterns of garden life. The short-wave was finally turned off after an unsuccessful attempt at listening to some light jazz. The drunken arguing of next-door neighbours was muffled by the carpet, as well as the excited shouts of the sports commentator from the football game the neighbour was watching in the next room. It got harder and harder to discern the fading colours as night fell, but you knew your path by heart, and you knew you were not going to fall asleep until your fingers had travelled all the way through the maze and triumphed in finding the narrow exit below the misshapen green bird in the far bottom corner by the piano. The journey was complete, and you could shut your eyes, hoping that the cheering for that last goal and the hysterical shrieks of the housewife next door, who was beaten by her drunken husband almost nightly, were going to blend into your wild dreams shortly.

38

Dear Sasha,

George, gone after staying as long as the night curfew for the Westerners allowed, would fall asleep in the international dorm, luxuriously designed to contain things like tiny fridges, individual desks and even television sets, but these fancy quarters were absolutely inaccessible to native students, like you, and were guarded closely by at least two attendants at all times.

You, dear Sasha, told us that these dorms were the same ones that had housed the university's first students three hundred years earlier, and that your great-great-grandfather used to board in them a century earlier. Your famous ancestor came from Siberia, the northern Russian territory where ethnic minorities were called *inorodtzy*, or people of non-Slavic origins. The word itself had a very negative connotation to it, as *inorodtzy* were citizens of the second class. Your great-great-grandfather was a state serf and was set free by the Emancipation Reform of the mid-nineteenth century.

He didn't have any formal schooling and had been taught to read by the village's deacon. After his mother's death and his father's subsequent marriage, he ran away from home at the age of fourteen, managing to pay for his travel all the way down to the capital by loading and unloading carriages and taking care of horses.

Being a big lad for his age, he managed to obtain an entrance to the Slavic department of the university, falsely claiming to be of Slavic origin, a deacon's son and seventeen years of age. He spent his days studying hard, working his way through by copying pages of the manuscript of the famous Professor Ivanov, *The Great Kievan Russia and Its History*. He ended up being one of Ivanov's favourite students, thus forever becoming the family's hero and even the founder of the familial academic scholarship.

39

Dear Sasha,

When both you and George were tired of telling your stories to me almost nightly sitting around the dinner table, mine followed. I would remember things from my childhood that I thought were long forgotten. Certain things you, dear Sasha, or George would mention in one of your stories – a splash of colour, a sound or a taste would bring back pictures from my past. Just like George's mention of the wooden coat stands in the university's library made me remember the wooden coat stand sitting in the corner of my primary school classroom.

I could tell who was in or out by glancing at it during almost all months of the year except the hottest two weeks of August, when no one wore a coat. The coats were hung on top of each other according to who was first in class on a particular morning. As these were times when hardly anyone could afford more than one type of outerwear a season, I would quickly get used to seeing the grey woollen coat belonging to our teacher, Mr Morris, and a number of shades of pink or purple or red belonging to the girls: Natalie's with smudges of paint from always playing around construction sites, as her father worked on those; Kathy's with missing buttons and frayed cuffs, as she had lost her mother while we were still in year two; Lizzy's with traces of mud and dog hair, as she had to walk to school for almost an hour every day and got a chance to pet all the stray dogs on the way; Marina's bright pink, freshly dry-cleaned coat whose smell was the envy of the classroom – Marina's mother ran a launderette.

I ended up seeing quite a bit of Lizzy and Natalie through the years, actually even dancing at Lizzy's wedding. I found out one morning that she was getting married to her beau, of whom no one in the family approved, when a thick envelope dropped through our letterbox with Lizzy's name on it. I was not a fan of weddings, having barely survived a recent church event of a family member, with memories of being bored to tears, frozen to the bone and worn out by the length of the service. However, we were fairly close with Lizzy, and I could not refuse her.

I danced almost non-stop, primarily to avoid looking at the distressed groom with utter disappointment, as I quickly realised why Lizzy's family was so much against him. He was rather characterless, with thin features, eyes of very pale blue, thin bones, and otherwise of very unpleasant demeanour. I wasn't quite sure why Lizzy had decided to venture into this relationship, but all of us have reasons for entering into such quick unions, whether it is pregnancy, a desire to show your ex that you are happy against all odds or some other open or hidden agenda.

I ended up dancing late into the night, quite unusually for me, as I was not dance floor material but rather preferred to sit at a table and talk politics with the old men with cigars. I even ended up dancing the tango, instructed right on the floor by Lizzy's great-uncle, who seemed to be as unsettled as I was about the affair. Our tango looked rather disturbing. I was clumsy and awkward, and Lizzy's great-uncle was wobbly and lost his balance every other step – not because he was a bad dancer, as later Lizzy assured me, but because he was hopelessly drunk that night, having just found out that his wife had been cheating on him for a number of years.

40

Dear Sasha,

Since you were raised by your grandmother far from the big city, your first visit to the city came when you were about the age of five. The scariest bit of the whole experience was stepping on the metro's escalator for the first time, this speedy moving staircase that threatened you the most. Your grandmother had talked to you about the 'magic moving steps' for a whole two weeks before the journey so that you could visualise in your five-year-old head how it would feel to step down into the underground in the crowd of other travellers, with flickering lights on both sides of the escalator and the sound of wind coming from the bottom, where the metro trains swallowed up and spat out other passengers, all apparently so at ease with the experience. Surrounded by disembarking passengers on all sides, you were rushed from the railway platform and through the metro's heavy doors, barely having any time to take a breath of frozen air and firm up your grasp on your grandmother's hand as she deposited a handful of orange coins with a clanking noise drowned out by the sound of adjacent entry gates. The whole thing sounded like the gambling hall at a Las Vegas hotel, which you, dear Sasha, could relate to many years from then.

The metal arm of the gate rotated, and you and your grandmother were pushed through by a beer-bellied man who positioned himself right behind the two of you. Frightened by the push, you ended up skipping a step and stumbling onto the escalator with your hands outstretched and your woollen boots with rubber bottoms sliding over the first few steps, and you crashed down on your bum. Your grandmother conveniently landed right next to you after jumping a few steps to catch you by the tassels of your winter scarf. The noises and the daylight quickly disappeared as you sped down the escalator, the longest escalator ride to the station so deep under the ground that you wondered whether you were getting closer to the centre of the earth.

41

Dear Sasha,

Sometimes you went quiet in the middle of an animated conversation, your smile fading. I would tug your sleeve, making a sad face and begging you to spill it out. And you reluctantly told us your sad stories, your memories of love affairs that were not meant to have happy endings, no matter the strength of the feelings of either party involved. These all revolved around your life in your university town, when you started and finished your mornings in the stuffy metro, squeezed between warmly dressed people in woollen or fur coats, and painfully stabbed in the thighs or stomach by angular briefcases of busy office workers. I used to nudge your neck with my nose, asking you to tell me more about the university, like how the building or the chapel looked.

'What chapel?' You laughed. 'You silly child, we are talking about Communist times, not Catherine the Great's reign!'

There was a little church nearby that the students had frequented before the revolution – as after the early 1920s, such visits were absolutely impossible – and if a student was found out to have visited the church for anything other than purely historical research, he or she would be expelled. But you, dear Sasha, always the one to get into mischief, excused your visits by flaunting a family history connection. You had once heard a family story about one Christmas from the times when your great-great-grandfather was a student there.

On that Christmas Eve, it was said that the organ master was playing with particular abandon while the students filled the rows and rows of dark brown seats, just like on all the previous years. The old wood made a squeaky noise every time someone took a seat with the particular impetuosity of a happy student on the last day before the holidays. One candle or another was relit every few minutes by a helpful third-year student with his gloves covered in melted paraffin wax.

The organ master was so involved in the music that he seemed to be ignorant of the fact that the chaplain was gesticulating passionately behind him and motioning him to stop. The chaplain finally had to touch the organ master's shoulder lightly and whisper something in his ear. The organ master jumped off the chair and ran out, pushing aside a few students on his route through the heavy wooden door.

The door shut noisily. That Christmas Eve, 1864, the carol service proceeded without the organ playing, as the organ master's wife had gone into labour and gave birth to a baby girl, the future wife of your great-great-grandfather.

Such was the family legend, but then, nobody knew if the details were true.

42

Dear Sasha,

Our evenings of storytelling were usually over by around the time good working people got out of bed to walk their dogs and have morning showers before waking their children and packing their lunches to go to work. George would be nodding off. You, dear Sasha, would be counting your cigarettes with a look of slight concern, realising that you had been smoking too much and had exceeded your day's average. I would begin clearing the table. I would glance up for a split second from watching my hands monotonously moving the breadcrumbs all the way to one side of the table, and my heart would sink, as it would be all over for the night, and you, dear Sasha, would shortly disappear into your room and not come out again until late morning. You would pause and glance back, studying my face. I would quickly fake a smile. 'Those foreigners, they don't tip whether sober or drunk,' I would say with a thick Irish accent. You, dear

Sasha, would burst out laughing, make your way back, grab and slightly tug my ear and then kiss me gently on the neck.

I knew you would only want this brief gesture of tenderness to be our goodnight kiss; thus, I would make a quick decision to drop to my knees and hug your thighs briskly before undoing your flies. I knew you could never refuse what was to follow, no matter how sleepy or sad or nostalgic for your former boyfriends you felt that night. My hands would shake slightly as I lowered your jeans and kissed the pale skin of your thighs just where your briefs ended and then move my lips higher. You would grab the edge of the table. I would work my lips and tongue higher and kiss your testicles and then quickly pull your briefs down and touch the end of your penis with my tongue. You would be erect, and your eyes would be firmly shut. I would take your penis in my mouth, working my lips up and down with my right hand massaging your buttocks.

George would be woken up, stretching, by the noise or the sense of something happening, his eyes widening with the excitement of an evening apparently still being very much on. I would know when to pause. Getting you to ejaculate too quickly would just end all the fun, so I would have to stop and move towards George and repeat the whole fellatio scenario all over again while you glared at me and George with your eyes glazed with a mixture of lust and something else, some kind of sadness.

I would usually know when to switch from one man to the other and come back to you again. I would hardly ever get to switch between you two more than twice before you grabbed me from behind, pushed me down on the table or the edge of the couch or a dining chair, pulled whatever I was wearing off and entered me from behind. You would be ever so gentle, proceed so slowly that I would hardly stand it, biting my lip. I knew that making any sounds would make you ejaculate quicker, so I would be as quiet as possible. I would hardly ever lose track of time, being way too conscious, not letting myself go and registering your every move, every breath and every touch of your hands on my shoulders, your fingers drawing invisible paintings on my back. My breathing would become shallow. Your moves would go from slow to very slow before you stopped abruptly, your grasp on my shoulders stiffening, and then you would start moving faster once more, and then you would stop again. Your grasp on my shoulders would slowly weaken. You would gently pull yourself out, tug my earlobe, touch my cheek, smudging a tear off my chin with one of your fingers, and then pull your jeans up with your usual 'You kids have fun; I will be off now' before leaving the room.

I would open my mouth to say something, but George, having patiently waited for you to finish, would grab me from behind and continue where you had left off. I would be a very different sexual partner with each of you. I would quickly get used to George's pace and manner – rougher than yours, even hostile at times. His movements were quick, his grasp on my body painful on occasion, but the red marks on my shoulders were only visible and felt later, as I could hardly concentrate on any sensations then, only wanting to be in the midst of this copulation and getting tired, really tired, so tired that I would fall asleep the moment my head hit the pillow.

So often, when George and I had finished and you, dear Sasha, were asleep in your bed, I would toss and turn while listening to the first commuters' cars starting their engines with George happily snoring next to me. You would sleep alone in your room on most nights no matter how we made love or whether we all ended up in our large bed together or did it in the dining room or the kitchen. On the days you fell asleep with the two of us, when we all fell into bed from sheer exhaustion and an overabundance of alcohol, you used to wake up in the middle of the night, gently pull your shoulder from under my cheek and leave the room, the heat of your body slowly disappearing and George's snoring becoming louder and more disturbing.

43

Dear Sasha,

I never felt welcome in your room. Whether it was the feeling that I was intruding into your personal space, which you only wanted to share with your thoughts and memories, firmly closing the door every time you wanted to separate your two worlds entirely, or whether it was the fact that I had never had my own room to begin with and thus never knew how it felt to claim my own space and be able to shut the door, I always felt a certain unpalatable sensation when I passed by the bolted and forbidden space.

I would sometimes enter your room when you were out, not to touch any of your personal belongings, of course, but just to sit still in there for a few moments in trying to understand what the feeling was all about. You, dear Sasha, never really locked yourself in except on a couple of occasions when we ended up fighting over one thing or another. You never actually said that George or I was not welcome in your room and even stated on a few occasions that we

104

shouldn't bother knocking. But when I did knock, you would open up with that look on your face, questioning my – or George's, for that matter – presence, a look similar to the one a neighbour you didn't really know the name of, having spoken to him twice in the previous year and both times about the weather, would give you…the look saying, 'And what can I do for you, stranger? Hopefully, it's nothing I will have to trouble myself with.'

That look would send my mind grasping for answers as to why you would be so distant suddenly while you were so close. I never felt that distance with George, and I don't think he ever felt it with me. No matter in which part of the flat we ended up barricading ourselves in with our thoughts or work, we somehow always left the side or even the front door to our personal space open. But you, dear Sasha, clearly drew the line between the time you shared with us and the time you chose not to.

44

Dear Sasha,

It was so windy that day that I had to close all the windows, but their frames still shook with the larger branches of the nearby tree violently banging on the glass, making me startle every time, interrupting what I was doing. I watched the tree shiver, tremble, sway back and forth and prepare for the next bluster. The wind would calm down for a minute or two, just enough for me to hear a faint chirping of the birds hiding deep in the branches, but then another gust would quiet the birds and send the branches pounding at the windows, swooshing with their leaves and scratching with their bark. You and George were working on your laptops, oblivious to the slam dance nature was performing for all of us two feet away from our noses. You two would not glance at or talk to each other, preferring messaging to any human interaction unless absolutely necessary.

I was tidying up but really just preferred to move from one part of the house to the next to see whether my mood or my ideas about what to do with the day would change depending on the angle from which I watched the two of you work. Watching your profiles made me feel much better than watching your backs. Somehow I felt melancholic when the only things I could see were occasional shoulder twitches or neck scratches. Your profiles seemed to make me more at peace with what was going on in the room, as well as distract me from the now-heavy rain adding a beatbox soundtrack to the cacophony.

George's face was thin, delicate. He pushed his lips together and bit the bottom one constantly. He slouched in his chair and glanced up now and then, staring blankly at the framed poster of the Royal Shakespeare Company's 1995 production of Chekhov's *The Cherry Orchard*. I was sure if I asked George whether he knew what we had hanging on the wall of our living room and what he stared at all day long every day, he would not be able to answer.

You, dear Sasha, had a more rounded face, your thick-framed glasses making you look like a primary school child studying for a maths test. I studied your face carefully. Yours was emotionless. I could not tell whether you were actually working on a project or catching up on your Facebook chats. You retained that poker face of a man who had had to keep his game private for many years – all your life, really. Your emotions always under control, quietly guarded, often withdrawn, you would react with the same reserved politeness to a question about your preferences for dinner as you would when I stood behind you and put my arms around your chest. I would nudge my nose and chin into your neck and kiss your shoulders one by one.

45

Dear Sasha,

Sometimes I felt that you regretted moving in with us. Sometimes I felt that you had done it out of necessity or convenience or curiosity. Whatever the reasons that made you consider being with us like this, so close, sharing the same living space, they must have included a longing for being cared for, pitied, loved and generally being fussed over rather than a desire to be a part of a family unit. You, dear Sasha, basically took the role of the child that George and I did not have. But I was afraid you were getting tired of that role, secretly wanting to be in a relationship with an equal or maybe even wanting to be a parent yourself, wanting to fuss over another person who would be weaker and in need of your many qualities, which George and I did not necessarily find that important in the day-to-day life race.

At first you, dear Sasha, were ecstatic at having my and George's ears at your disposal, ready to listen to anything that you had to say any time you were ready to share. This was how the roles in our relationship were dealt out. You talked. I listened and consoled. George nodded. I wiped your tears, and I was sure I created even more by prompting more conversations about the painful memories that you retrieved when we sat down for meals with a bottle of wine and a good view out of the dining room window. I loved you, and I thought the world of you, dear Sasha, and I admired everything you said or did. I told you that you managed well, that thousands committed suicide, drank themselves to death, ended up in psychiatric hospitals or prisons, but you, dear Sasha, survived being gay in one of the most unfavourable places on earth. You managed to love and be loved and withstand the hate and fear of your family, fear for your safety and of public condemnation and shame, hate for the fact that you were different, that you were 'abnormal' and that your family had to struggle to hide your abnormality from the rest of the community. I put into words everything that you suspected – knew, even – and so desperately wanted to hear from someone else.

You talked. George nodded. I listened. But when the night came, so did the feeling of homesickness for even the most intolerable of places and painful of memories, and these were also part of your home.

46

Dear Sasha,

It was past nine in the evening. End of May. It got dark very late. I could still see some traces of daylight around ten o'clock sometimes. I was waiting for a call or text from you, dear Sasha. You had gone back home 'to take care of some business'. You first flew from Heathrow to Kyiv. Then you took the train to your hometown of Gogol. George and I hadn't heard from you since you had taken off that morning. You had promised to text from the train station right before you boarded the train, but you did not. You were supposed to meet 'some friends' upon arrival, whom you 'hadn't seen in a while'. I waited until midnight and ended up going to bed, George tagging along with his book and two cups of tea.

You had a peculiar side, dear Sasha. You disconnected easily. I never quite understood how one could so quickly switch off after barely leaving someone just a few hours earlier. Of course, you were distracted by people and places, but there should be some kind of emotional responsibility for those who stay behind. They ought not to be forgotten, or at least they should be fooled into thinking they haven't been upon receiving the traveller's text confirming a safe landing. But there was nothing from you, dear Sasha, until the evening after.

The following two weeks, you communicated in bursts, sounding very distant, looking through me and straight into the kitchen behind my back while I was searching your face for signs of affection or at least warmth. Nothing of that sort came through the computer screen, but once, when you ended up drinking quite a bit and decided to tell me in English – making sure none of your relatives or friends present at that moment in your small flat in Gogol had a chance of understanding – that you missed me.

'It's your hands; you have magical hands,' you said, your accent coming straight from the black-and-white American films you had so carefully learned the language from.

'Our linguistic genius,' I called you, as you learned languages fast, often being able to fully explain yourself and have a decent conversation on almost any topic after reading just one book in that language. You could read, write and speak Russian, Ukrainian, Polish, Spanish, Italian, French, German and English. Your personal record, of course, paled in comparison with such polyglots as the eighteenth-century Italian cardinal Giuseppe Mezzofanti, who spoke thirty-nine languages, or the nineteenth-century Hong Kong governor Sir John Bowring, who knew two hundred of them. However, your fluency in eight languages and your ability to change freely between them was impressive nonetheless and was a huge turn-on for me.

47

Dear Sasha,

As your absence would slowly come to an end, the frequency of your communication with us would invariably increase. You would switch gears. The messages would become more detailed, and there would be eagerness in your voice. I could feel that you had had your homeland fix and were ready to come back. And so you would, on a sunny day in early June or a not-so-sunny one in late September or a predictably soggy early afternoon in mid-December, when I would run towards you at Heathrow and almost knock you off your feet, covering you with kisses and hugging you tightly while George stood back with a wide smile. You would let yourself be squeezed and loved for a good half a minute before making a weak attempt at freeing yourself, looking at me with the satisfaction of a cat who has had a successful hunt and is pleased to climb back through the kitchen window to discover a newly opened tin of food and a bowl of fresh water ready for his enjoyment.

No wonder, dear Sasha, you got along with our cat, James, so nicely. You might have been related, after all. Your manners were catlike. You would walk lightly, scaring me by switching sides of the room without a single sound. Sometimes I would feel that you, dear Sasha, did not really love me or George; you just loved the fact that your food bowl was always full.

48

Dear Sasha,

Late one evening, we were driving along a rural road, looking left and right for a sign pointing to a hotel or an inn or a guest house of any kind just to get ourselves out of the car and onto a bed or couch of any sort so we could put our feet up. Finally we noticed an arrow with the word INN and a picture of a house, only to realise after slowing down that the building was half-demolished. Part of it had burned down, and the other part was slowly deteriorating from the elements and the lack of care. The sign was still very much upright and readable – FOUR CROSSES INN. Part of a wall that was still standing had four crosses painted in black, chipped but still prominent.

I parked the car, closed my eyes and leaned back. I was too tired to drive any further. After we had piled out of the car one after another into the vacant car park, you and George circled the house, exchanging sarcastic comments about whether we were going to find a room that was intact enough to give us shelter for the night. The headlights of the car illuminated two tired, slouching figures moving around and peeking through broken windows. I wondered what would happen if I were to switch off the lights. How would the two of you find your way in and out of this wreck of an inn?

I drifted off and was woken up by you, dear Sasha, patting my shoulder lightly and almost yelling in my ear, 'You will not believe it, but I just Googled this place, and it's ancient. Jonathan Swift used to stop here, and imagine, just imagine, this inn actually used to be called Three Crosses once, but then Swift had a run-in with the wife of the inn-keeper. Very much pissed with the rudeness of the landlady, he engraved a poem with his diamond ring on the window pane.'

At this point, dear Sasha, you actually decided to consult your phone to make sure you quoted correctly. '"You have three crosses on your door; hang up your wife, and she'll make four." Isn't it fantastic?'

Poor Sasha, you were born and raised in a country that demolished its historical buildings and erased and rewrote its history before the Communist revolution, thus denying its citizens this kind of simple pleasure – finding a few-hundred-year-old inn with some connection to a famous writer and actually being able to touch the half-burnt walls.

49

Dear Sasha,

The most difficult thing is to accept that it is over.

>ME: Are you missing me?
>YOU: Very much. Some days.

Part of you hopes that you can salvage the wreck.

>ME: How are you getting on there?
>YOU: I manage. Still alive.

But part of you, the more realistic one, knows that you shouldn't.

>ME: Are you ever coming back?
>YOU: I can't.

But you hang on.

ME: *(Crying)* Sasha!
YOU: *(Silence)*

And on.

ME: *(Sobbing)* Sasha!
YOU: *(Silence)*

And on.

ME: *(Whispering)* Sasha!
YOU: *(Silence)*

Then you give up.

ME: I love you.
YOU: I'd better go.

50

Dear Sasha,

Depression hit when I least expected it, right after the move was over, and I had just a few boxes left to unpack and a need to plan out which shelves to use for the medicine cabinet and which ones for the cans of tomato sauce and baked beans.

I had anticipated waking up the morning after the movers had left – energetic and muscly Eastern European types, blonde-haired and blue-eyed – and indulging in the nesting routine of discovering things about the new place that I might have missed the first time around, like a dryer function on a washing machine, wooden blinds – I hate plastic ones – lots of room to hang pictures in the long, narrow corridor and a whole bunch of cute cups with pictures of bunnies and hedgehogs apparently left by the previous tenants.

But I woke up feeling numb inside, my muscles aching, my chest hurting so that I could hardly take a breath. I knew it was not my heart. It was my *heart*...

We moved into the country once you left, dear Sasha. There was no use keeping the London flat – it felt too spacious for just the two of us and a cat. The country sounded like fun. It sounded like a change. A fresh start and a view of cows and lambs through the window. So far had we got away from the city, actually, that it would now take us at least an hour and a half to get into London. But I suddenly did not want the city – the city was bothering me on a hot Saturday with all its residents suddenly out with loud voices and lots of uncovered, white, flabby flesh. They would peek out of honking cars or shout at the pedestrian versions of themselves while they were trying to cross the hot streets.

I broke into a sweat trying to navigate my way to the shops to fetch a last-minute snack before jumping in the car to follow our moving van out of the city and onto the M1. And I was glad to be out. I was very happy to be leaving London and was very happy to settle in a new house, until this morning. I recognised the feeling immediately, when my chest felt crushed, when I was not able to take a full breath and smile at the joke George threw at me after opening Facebook and taking the first sip from his morning coffee. I didn't like this feeling. It was going to be a long and painful few months. I was going to be mourning the loss of a friend.

51

Dear Sasha,

The first photo I saw of you was the one at your graduation. Shortish. Stocky. Grey woollen blazer and trousers of the same colour. Nothing more adventurous was allowed, as if wearing a blazer of a slightly darker colour than the trousers could have any effect on one's Communist consciousness. Your shoes were not in the picture. But all twenty-three-year-olds were wearing black lacquered shoes and grey woollen suits at their graduations, and then at all the functions following them into the later years of their lives. And assuming one hadn't grown a particularly pudgy beer tummy in one's mid-forties, one could easily fit into one's graduation suit all the way through to one's retirement party. Some, I have heard, were buried in the suits they were married in.

I have snapped the picture with my iPhone. Now I have a digitally enhanced black-and-white photo of a twenty-three-year-old you, dear Sasha, standing on the stage of a university concert hall more than a quarter of a century ago.

Shoulder-length blonde hair, your fringe almost covering your whole face – or so it appeared, as you were looking down at a piece of paper in your hands, presumably the graduation ceremony's programme. When you are ready to fall in love, nothing can stand in your way, not even the fact that you don't know the colour of your beloved's eyes.

52

Dear Sasha,

I fell in love enough times in my late teens and early twenties to realise that I had just about had enough inoculations and then boosters to prevent any future illnesses. That is why, at the age of twenty-five, I cool-headedly decided to settle down and ever since have been enjoying my married life with George, having decided pretty much the course of my life all the way through to old age.

One day, I would have children. And then one day, the children would grow up, and I would hopefully have only a few years' break before fully involving myself in raising the grandchildren while having an occasional holiday in France with George or a weekend away with a steady set of girl-friends.

It just so happened that the inoculations wore out. Some-how I managed to get sick again, and the disease turned out to be as disastrous as a case of measles in an adult.

53

Dear Sasha,

Tangerines, available in your childhood only around December and January and acquired only after queuing for hours in the freezing cold outside fruit-and-vegetable kiosks, were carefully sewn together and placed around the branches of the New Year's tree – called so as Christmas was forbidden as a religious holiday and all the gift-giving and the drinking were done on 31 December. The smell of the fruit would wrestle with the smell of the fir. Tangerines always won year after year, you told me, dear Sasha, as the firs, cut fresh in mid-December, were losing their needles and scent by early January. The trees were supposed to be kept all the way until 14 January – New Year's Day according to the old Ukrainian calendar. By then, the floor was covered with yellowing needles and dried-up tangerine skins.

54

Dear Sasha,

As European cinema was allowed and tolerated in Communist Russia, however censored, photos of French and Italian film stars were carefully cut out by you and your brother and taped to the opposite walls of the bedroom you shared in the state-owned flat in the suburbs of Gogol.

Above your bed, Gérard Depardieu, Pierre Richard, Michele Placido, Louis de Funès and somehow Michael Douglas – an American from one of a handful of US films that got through the Iron Curtain during the Cold War – were staring at Sophia Loren, Catherine Deneuve and Sophie Marceau on the opposite wall, above your brother's. An aged piano and a desk with two piles of schoolbooks on each side were all the room could fit. You sat at the desk for long stretches of time, sweating over maths, Ukrainian, Russian, English, German…until you had collected all the excellent marks you could manage from praising teachers. Your brother barely opened his books. Being from the troubled generation of lost youth of the sixties, he claimed that he did not need 'all this academia'.

'I will emigrate to the West and become a businessman,' he said. And he did. So the only thing he actually used in your shared bedroom was his bed. The only times he used it was at bedtime. The rest of the day he spent buying and selling whatever he could get his hands on and whatever had any resale potential in a country plagued by shortages of every product imaginable, bars of soap one week, boxes of matches the next.

There wasn't much of the flat to remember. Kitchen table: white, peeling, a green stain in the middle where you had decided to paint your year-five art project. The water-colours had soaked through the paper, and you were grounded for the evening, which meant being forbidden from watching the fifteenth episode of the country's favourite World War II drama.

Four chairs. When the whole family sat down to dinner, there was little space to squeeze yourselves in. You were propped up by the sink, a cabinet and a cooker. Wet sheets, shirts and trousers would be dried up on ropes stretched from just over the cooker on one side of the kitchen to above the fridge on the other side. The drying laundry covered the windows. The family had its meals in silence. *When you eat your meals, you are deaf and mute* – the old saying used to be taught from early toddlerhood to every Ukrainian child. The saying actually rhymed in your native language.

55

Dear Sasha,

The first McDonald's in Gogol was opened with a music band playing national anthem music and Gogol's mayor cutting the red ribbon by the main entrance. You and your brother queued up for an hour and a half around the town's central square while the thermometers were hovering around minus twenty degrees Celsius, the queue four to five people thick going around the perimeter. Your first hamburger was the most delicious capitalist food you had ever tasted. The second and the third ones and then the helping of 129fries finally warmed you boys up.

'Memories brought by senses,' you once said while helping yourself to a burger in a less famous London fast-food joint, unforgettably claiming that your brain lights up like a monk's MRI during meditation when you taste something that reminds you of your childhood.

56

Dear Sasha,

Vodka. You were ten. Your father decided to introduce you to the taste of the famous national beverage. Your tongue burned. As you found out later, you were supposed to gulp it straight down your throat in one shot. No tongues.

57

Dear Sasha,

Alexander is the English version of your name, which is of Greek origin and is very much used around the world in various transliterations – Alex, Shura…Alexander the Great was the name you called yourself in your early teens, and you thought of it as a plausible version of your name and even a useful Westernised version of it, as you were determined one day to bed the British prince Edward, the Queen's third son, who showed up in Ukraine one day to promote theatre arts. Never happened.

58

Dear Sasha,

The waters were receding slowly, uncovering the sand and whatever was trapped in it – shells, a couple of beer bottles, a round red buoy, a second one, and a third, a forgotten beach chair, a dog's toy, a child's toy, the remains of a surf-board, black rocks glistening in the light of the full moon. It felt like someone was in charge of pushing the water aside forcefully, with the waters pulling right back.

The water-commanding superhuman, however, was slowly winning, metre by metre, until nearly all the 250 me-tres of distance on the south coast of Devon was clear, sand wet but perfectly walkable all the way to the island and back to the fishing village. A perfect mourning place for aban-doned lovers or the ones who chose to be abandoned and do some of the abandoning themselves by pushing away the ones they were afraid of losing.

When your crying is in sync with the seagulls, then you know the place works for post-break-up periods. I hadn't been given enough time to love you. You were like a dish barely tasted that was rudely whisked away by a waiter while I was still holding my fork over it, reaching for the most delicious bites. I was left hungry for all the sensations, excitement, exhilaration and turmoil I could still experience if you had still been here. But not being a masochistic type, one who is quite practical in her love affairs, I cut our affair short and put you, dear Sasha, on the plane back home without a single tear. I scheduled my wisdom tooth operation the same afternoon, conveniently loading myself with painkillers en route. Once the painkillers wore off at dinnertime, the pain burst out.

59

Dear Sasha,

Unfortunately, my drinking years happened long after my father's death; thus, we had nothing in common during my childhood and adolescence. I don't remember him actively engaging in any activity other than drinking. He did drink while watching sports on the telly, so I guess if I had kept on top of the football and hockey scores, we could have found some common topics for conversation, but I never seemed to find myself drawn to watching sports beyond opening and closing ceremonies for Olympic Games.

So, dear Sasha, I did have flashbacks of my father's downing a bottle of vodka while George, you and I shared our bottle of Grey Goose or Smirnoff on occasion, and I feel that I do understand him better now, knowing how heartache tastes after a shot or two or three…

I am guessing, however, that my father, the old-fashioned kind of guy he was, wouldn't have approved of me now any more than he did back when I was in my teens. For him, my poetry writing and boyfriend hopping was too much of a bohemian thing. I am guessing if he were alive now and I were to tell him after sharing a bottle with him that I slowed down, settled and lived with two men I loved greatly, he would flip.

60

Dear Sasha,

Because of the faults in road construction or the shifting of tectonic plates, the puddle near our house never completely dries up. Of course, the rain tops it up every couple of days, but even if the weather is miraculously dry for a few days at a time, the puddle remains there. It is convenient for calculating the strength of the current rain, as sometimes the drops on the windows are not a good indicator of the velocity of the water coming down from the sky. *Is the hooded raincoat enough? Or should I take an umbrella? The smallish, cheapie one or the more durable that should also survive the wind?*

This very puddle reminds me of another one – or a family of them, actually – that surrounded our apartment block season in and out during my childhood. These bodies of water were not just essential indicators of the weather but also, more importantly, eternal playgrounds with a multitude of possibilities for the children to entertain themselves.

Guessing whose handmade boat could survive the journey across the biggest puddle was the most common game in the neighbourhood. Measuring the depth of the puddles by walking right through them barefoot in the summers was a more daredevil activity, which could only be topped by walking on the first layer of ice and watching it crackle or wading with a stick in the dark and murky water, trying to find abandoned treasures like an open tuna can or a drenched pack of cigarettes.

I distinctly remember that those puddles always irritated the adults and pleased the children. A twice-a-day walk around on the way to school and back presented a multitude of opportunities, and if one were in a rush, just stopping by for a split second and seeing one's own reflection or that of the sky was pleasing entertainment in the pre-internet age.

I am watching our new puddle right now for signs of rain. It drizzles. Then stops. The passing cars nearly touch its edge, leaving most of it perfectly still.

61

Dear Sasha,

I feel like I have to live a certain number of lives simultaneously to feel alive. The one I am leading now, a quiet suburban one in an English village with twice-weekly shopping trips to Sainsbury's and an occasional charity shop tour in the nearby small town, is barely enough to get me to a quarter of my living potential. I am emotionally capable and even in desperate need of having another life, imaginary most of the time but with occasional real-person input, a short chat or a text or a message in my inbox accompanied by a morning coffee, something to keep me dreaming and sane.

62

Dear Sasha,

The psychology of nostalgia is best portrayed as the 'ratatouille effect' in a Disney film about a gifted rat concocting a restaurant-quality dish for a stern food critic. The grim critic suddenly stops in his tracks, the taste of the first bite he takes filling his nostrils and his soul with the longing and nostalgia for the smells and tastes of times when those meant comfort and contentment in his mother's cooking.

The time machine that is initiated inside your brain is magical and real at the same time. The sensations are euphoric. The most unpleasant or mundane smells – like old lorry exhausts, the nausea-provoking stench from a urine-soaked rug used as a toilet by generations of felines in cheap housing estates on the city edge, the faint rusty scent and rhythmic sounds of train tracks, the various odours of underground stations with their twists and turns and tunnels squeezing the crowds through, with their narrowness and overflowing rubbish bins, the burning, curious looks of stray cats jumping from under car tyres, various aromas that hit you on entering shops – that surround you mess with your brain and don't let you go until you have surrendered yourself to this time machine. You feel the sense of dread when the scent and the memory it brought with it are gone, leaving you with the nauseous feeling of the doom that reality is.

63

Dear Sasha,

You said that Westerners have not perfected a simple skill that is indispensable in the East – eating a ripe tomato. You said that our tomatoes are firm and meaty and have no juice in them, and eating them is an easy game. But try eating a ripe tomato, you said, with juice bursting out the moment you touch the red flesh with your lips, hours after these fruits have been picked by farmers from their tiny gardens and sold from aluminium bowls alongside the motorway stretching between Gogol and Kyiv. You said you have to approach such a tomato with the tenderness and cautiousness with which you would approach your first kiss. You said you have to hold the tomato just above your mouth, your head tilted back before your first bite, and when you carefully place your teeth on the fruit, you have to bite in slowly, letting the juice drip into your mouth, sucking it in and then biting deeper. You said you have to proceed by slightly tilting the tomato left and right and biting small bits and drinking

141

whatever juice comes out until you are left with nothing but the mushy flesh and some skin. You said that the experts – and you were one of them! – do stop now and then and manage even to sprinkle some salt before taking the next bite without splashing any juice on their light-coloured shirts. The experts even manage to have a bite of toast, which usually patiently sits on a plate next to a shot of vodka. You said these ripe tomatoes make vodka taste better. I said that nothing makes vodka taste better than kissing you right after taking a shot.

64

Dear Sasha,

I was walking the streets of the sleeping city yesterday, noting the lit windows in grey blocks of flats: a couple here, a couple there, none in this five-storey, fairly modern one except a faint night light behind the blinds – somebody was scared of sleeping in the dark, probably a child. The lit windows housed the still-awake residents, some working on their laptops, some having nightcaps, some arguing, some waiting to take a night cab to an airport, some waiting for loved ones to come back home from a night shift.

I wonder if anybody questioned the light in our window all the way back last year, when we stayed up until the early hours of the morning more times than I can remember. I wonder if anybody wondered.

I couldn't sleep last night. As tired as I was and as tightly as I tried to close my eyes and as still as I tried to lie in bed, I just couldn't fall asleep. After tossing and turning for an hour and a half, I put my coat on and left the house to roam the nearby streets and stare at people's windows. None of the ground-floor flats were lit, so I had to make do with fantasising about the happenings behind the curtains and the shades and the blinds of all the windows higher up.

I wonder if you slept well yesterday, dear Sasha.

65

Dear Sasha,

I found a note from the postman stuck in our gate today:

You've got a parcel, but it was too big to fit in your letterbox, and you were not at home. I will be walking around the village between 11.30 and 1.30 if you want to find me and collect your parcel.

It was quarter to two, but even if I had managed to come home a bit earlier, I do not think I would have fancied running through the village in the pouring rain, trying to spot the postman's van. I sat down heavily on the kitchen stool without taking my coat off, trying to figure out what the postman could have delivered to me today that I would have to wait for until tomorrow. A pair of pyjamas I have ordered from a catalogue? No, a bit early, I thought. They wouldn't ship them out that fast. A two-factor authentication device to log in to my bank account? Mine has developed a flickering screen, and I've had to guess the code digits the last few times I've used it, so I called up the bank and ordered a new one. That must be it.

Or maybe it is an early Christmas present from someone that I know, either locally or internationally. I have in the past received gift baskets out of nowhere and then struggled to attach a face to the name on the gift card. I often make a random order on Amazon or eBay and then forget all about it until the package comes in, and I am pleasantly surprised if the item matches the picture or unpleasantly surprised if it does not. I hate filling out the return slips and going to our local post office, which has lately had the most annoying habit of replacing the clerks the moment they find out the difference between the first-class and the recorded second-class services.

I played around with the postman's note and wondered why on earth he hadn't left the parcel sitting next to our door. From what I know about our village, none of its inhabitants, most of them pushing eighty, would be so adventurous as to steal someone's parcel on their way to the village pub or back home, struggling to retain a grip on their dog's leash. But our postman must have thought otherwise. In any case, I have to wait until tomorrow to be surprised.

66

Dear Sasha,

My hairdresser knew it all. He was an intelligent fellow, and he knew what I wanted to become, depending on my facial expression the moment I walked through the door. If I was looking more or less like a female who had made an effort to look like one, Paul knew that he had to try to make me more feminine on that particular occasion. The days I showed up dishevelled, wearing a pair of torn jeans and an old T-shirt, Paul pulled his sharpest scissors out and knew that he had to cut it short. 'Boy short, please.'

On special occasions, Paul could feel that I missed you, and he looked at me with the sad smile of a gay hairdresser who knew the drill – girl meets boy; girl realises boy is gay; girl tries to look like a boy by getting very, very, very short haircuts.

Dear Sasha, I imagine you would have loved Paul. I imagine you and Paul would have made a lovely pair, and if I had walked into the salon with you in tow, Paul would have done a poor job styling my hair, as he would have looked your way half the time while you pretended to read an article in last year's edition of *Style* magazine about one celebrity or another coming out, falling in love, marrying or divorcing, or having babies. But I never brought you to visit Paul with me. I needed Paul's full attention on my thin, greying locks. And I needed him to look into my eyes, both of us facing his large oval mirror, and I needed Paul to tell me, 'All will be okay,' although we both knew that it wouldn't.

67

Dear Sasha,

I allow myself to eat comfort food on rainy days without feeling much guilt about it. A buttered toasted teacake goes very well with light drizzles. Much heavier rains require banoffee pie or at least a scone with some strawberry jam and clotted cream.

You had your own recipes for rainy days, dear Sasha. Vodka followed by fried potatoes with onions and mushrooms did wonders for gloomy moods inspired by gloomy weather. I have tried to make this dish just the way you made it. I can't. I slice the potatoes too thinly, and I put too much oil in the frying pan, so my potatoes are much too soaked in it, and I never could keep the ratio of potatoes and mushrooms and onions as perfect as you did. But on rainy days, after going through the sweets and cakes and after unsuccessfully trying to warm myself up with a seventh cup of tea, I get the peeler and hope for the best. Five shots of vodka later, my dish of mushy fried potatoes tastes just fine.

Acknowledgements

First and foremost, a heartfelt thank you to George and Sasha. Though society, with its prejudices and unfair laws, once tore you apart, you found each other again (well, with my help, please don't forget this, guys) and created a love story for the ages.

To my friends and family who supported me through this whirlwind of emotions, thank you for not bolting when things got complicated. Your love, laughter, and endless supply of tissues have been amazing.

A big shoutout to Ockham Publishing Group and Rob Johnson, its commissioning editor, who took a chance on this unconventional tale and helped it find its second home after its journey with the first publisher was cut short by financial shenanigans. Rest assured, their collapse had nothing to do with this memoir.

To my mother, Gala, who passed on to me the thirst for love and creative writing, and to my daughter, Shelly, who will undoubtedly outshine me as a writer and probably win the Pulitzer one day while casually sipping her morning tea, crocheting her masterpieces, listening to an audiobook on women's rights, running for MP from the Green Party, and editing her PhD at the same time.

To the readers and critics who embraced the first edition of this book with open arms and mind and made it a best-seller almost 10 years ago. Your kind words and thoughtful critiques have been the heartbeat of this journey. Your appreciation of our quirky, heartfelt story has made every tear-soaked pillow and belly laugh worth it.

And to the global LGBTQ+ community, this one's for you. Your stories, struggles, and triumphs are the soul of this memoir. May we all find the courage to love openly, live authentically, and never shy away from dancing to our own beat, even if the music gets a little off-key.

With gratitude, laughter, and a heart full of love,

Julie G. Fox

www.ingramcontent.com/pod-product-compliance
Lightning Source LLC
Chambersburg PA
CBHW031623040426
42452CB00007B/639